United Methodist Questions,
United Methodist Answers

United Methodist Questions, United Methodist Answers

Exploring Christian Faith

F. Belton Joyner Jr.

Westminster John Knox Press
LOUISVILLE • LONDON

Scripture quotations from the New Revised Standard Version of the Bible are copyright © 1989 by the Division of Christian Education of the National Council of the Churches of Christ in the U.S.A. and are used by permission.

Book design by Sharon Adams
Cover design by Night & Day Design

First edition
Published by Westminster John Knox Press
Louisville, Kentucky

This book is printed on acid-free paper that meets the American National Standards Institute Z39.48 standard. ∞

PRINTED IN THE UNITED STATES OF AMERICA

07 08 09 10 11 12 13 14 15 16 — 10 9 8 7 6 5 4 3 2 1

Library of Congress Cataloging-in-Publication Data is on file at the Library of Congress, Washington, D.C.

ISBN-13: 978-0-664-23039-5
ISBN-10: 0-664-23039-3

With gratitude for my journey with three lifelong United Methodists,
Peggy Ann, Mary Beth, and Bob,
and with appreciation for Diane, who has been a good United Methodist
ever since she joined this denominational journey

Contents

Contents

13 Polity   106

Welcome to the Book

QUESTIONS

The Bible is crawling with questions. Almost every page has somebody asking something about something! "Did God say, 'You shall not eat from any tree in the garden'?" (Gen. 3:1). "If I come to the Israelites and say to them, 'The God of your ancestors has sent me to you,' and they ask me, 'What is his name?' what shall I say to them?" (Exod. 3:13). "What will one answer the messengers of the nation?" (Isa. 14:32). "O LORD, how long shall I cry for help, and you will not listen?" (Hab. 1:2). "How can this be, since I am a virgin?" (Luke 1:34). "And who is my neighbor?" (Luke 10:29). "But who do you say that I am?" (Matt. 16:15).

In some ways, the biblical revelation is a rhythm of questions and answers. And if you and I had been there, we would have added our own questions! Maybe it helps to think of the church as "the community of questions" more than as "the community of answers." The attitude of question suggests movement, openness, and next steps. Keep on asking; it is good evidence that you are not dead!

As I developed this series of questions and answers, I kept on thinking of more things to ask and of more things to say in reply, but the editors did not think that a fourteen-volume collection would be as helpful as this more accessible version! (I still wish I had said more about "perfection" in answering question 53, and wish I had distinguished between doctrine and theology in question 49!)

THIS BOOK

The pattern of the book is to ask a question and then to give a United Methodist response. I am well aware that I do not speak for all ten million United Methodists, so I have tried to put my answers in terms of the United Methodist standards of doctrine (see question 49) and in light of *The Book of Discipline 2004* (see question 73). Frequently, there is reference to a relevant biblical passage. After each answer, I have called on the United Methodist heritage of theology in hymns by quoting from the hymns of Charles Wesley (see question 67). The language is poetic and sometimes reflects eighteenth-century English usage, but the words capture the heart of United Methodist teaching. All the hymns are found in *The United Methodist Hymnal*; at the end of this book, there is a list of the hymn numbers used.

My answers do not end the dialogue. Questions seem to lead to more questions, so I have ended each section with a question for your further reflection. Some of these questions can be answered fairly simply just from your own experience; some of the questions seek harder-to-find responses. These additional queries represent the continuing conversation of Christian theology.

It is hard for me as a Christian with a lifelong journey in the traditions of United Methodism to avoid assuming that "Well, everybody knows that." When I think you might want a quick reference point for a definition or clarification, I have noted "See question—." Perhaps this thumbing back and forth within the book will keep confusion to a minimum.

United Methodism is within the larger flow of the Christian church. We hold much in common with brothers and sisters in other traditions, but there are distinctive emphases that have shaped us. This book will sometimes pull from the universal Christian heritage and will sometimes draw from the well of United Methodist distinctiveness.

SOURCES

Throughout the book, I have referred to some basic United Methodist sources. The Articles of Religion and the Confession of Faith (see question 49) and the General Rules (see questions 31 and 35) and other official statements are found in *The Book of Discipline*

2004 (see question 73). (This is *The Book of Discipline of The United Methodist Church 2004* [Nashville: United Methodist Publishing House, 2004].)

The quotations from the sermons and other writings of John Wesley (Methodist roots) come from *The Works of John Wesley,* ed., Albert Outler, vol. 1 (Nashville: Abingdon Press, 1984); vol. 2 (Nashville: Abingdon Press, 1985); and vol. 3 (Nashville: Abingdon Press, 1986); and *The Works of John Wesley,* ed. Rupert Davies, vol. 9 (Nashville: Abingdon Press, 1989). There are fewer quotations from Philip William Otterbein, Martin Boehm, and Jacob Albright (see question 67) of the Evangelical United Brethren background because these men left almost no written documents.

Hymns and references to services of worship are taken from the hymnal (*The United Methodist Hymnal* [Nashville: United Methodist Publishing House, 1989]). There are also items from the worship book (*The United Methodist Book of Worship* [Nashville: United Methodist Publishing House, 1992]).

Quotations from John Wesley's commentary on the New Testament come from his *Explanatory Notes* (John Wesley, *Explanatory Notes upon the New Testament* (n.d.; repr., Naperville; IL: Alec R. Allenson, 1958). This material can also be searched on the Internet.

There are suggestions for further reading on p. 121 of this book.

ABBREVIATIONS

For convenience, sources used frequently have been abbreviated, especially in parenthetic references.

UNITED METHODIST SOURCES

BOD   *The Book of Discipline 2004*
BOW   *The United Methodist Book of Worship*
UMH   *The United Methodist Hymnal*

BOOKS OF JOHN WESLEY

Explanatory Notes   *Explanatory Notes upon the New Testament*
Works   *The Works of John Wesley*

HOW TO USE THIS BOOK

If a Sunday school class or other study group wants to go through these questions together, it might set aside thirteen weeks (a quarter of the year). There are thirteen chapters, one for each week of the quarter. Members could covenant to read a question a day for six days and then come together on the seventh day to share learnings, doubts, and new questions. A possible outline for such discussion might be the series of "Another question" at the end of each section.

An individual using this book might choose to skip and dip, following his or her own line of interest. Discussing the follow-up question with a friend will enrich the reading. Of course, I also invite you to read the book straight through, probably marking the margins with howls of protest and exclamations of agreeing joy!

ONE OTHER THING

This book comes on the heels of a volume published by Geneva Press, *Presbyterian Questions, Presbyterian Answers*. I am grateful to author Donald K. McKim for letting me bounce off his excellent insights. Occasionally, Don, I stole shamelessly, but I hope I hid it well enough to claim it for my own! Maybe this connection reflects the gracious gift of God in the larger family of faith. To God be the glory.

1

God

 1. How do we know God?

What we know about God is what God has revealed to us. Human understanding of God is limited by the boundaries of human imagination and vocabulary. God is beyond human capacity. God is "wholly other." Sometimes this is referred to as the transcendence of God.

God has taken the initiative to be known by humankind. The biblical word for this kind of knowledge has a quality of intimacy and closeness. God is here. Sometimes this is referred to as the immanence of God.

The full expression of God is in Jesus Christ. (See question 2 and question 7.) No wonder that Jesus is called Emmanuel—that name means "God with us" (Matt. 1:23). God cares so much about what is happening among humans that God came and lived among us. That tells us something about God!

Ages ago, people who responded to God's loving presence began to keep a record of what God did among God's people. Stories were told. Poems were written. Laws were noted. Events were remembered. Teachings were traced. Testimonies were recalled. Legends were transmitted. Judgments were heard. Hope was depicted. People of faith began to recognize that these records of God's work were themselves revelation from God. So we say that the Bible is another way we get to know God (2 Tim. 3:16). (See question 43.)

United Methodists tend to put an emphasis on a personal experience with God. A preacher might say: "It is not enough to know about God; one must know God." This personal experience is sometimes active in the obvious ("God has made the orchid a thing of beauty!"), which might be called general revelation. This personal experience is sometimes companion only to the gift of faith, which might be called special revelation. In this regard, United Methodists often celebrate the experience of founder John Wesley (see question 67) who wrote in his May 24, 1738, journal about what happened when he went to what was probably a Moravian small-group meeting at Aldersgate Street in London: "About a quarter before nine, while [the reader] was describing the change which God works in the heart through faith in Christ, I felt my heart strangely warmed. I felt I did trust in Christ, Christ alone, for salvation; and an assurance was given me, that He had taken away my sins, even mine, and saved me from the law of sin and death." Out of such encounters with the movement of God, we get to know God.

> Spirit of faith, come down, reveal the things of God,
> and make to us the Godhead known.

Another question: What is the difference between knowing about God and knowing God?

2. Who is the Trinity?

The simplest answer to this question is: "God." "Trinity" is the term the church uses to convey the reality that God exists in three persons; the traditional language for these three persons is "Father, Son, and Holy Spirit." These persons are coequal and coeternal. They mutually dwell in each other.

This description of "three persons" may sound like three gods. Not so! There is one living God. Theologians say that these three persons are of one substance. That means they are of one nature, one essence, one being. (That nature is love.) That is why the church proclaims there is one God.

The Bible does not use the word "Trinity," but the revelation of the three persons of the Godhead shows up in the Scripture. (For example, look at Matt. 28:19; 2 Cor. 13:13; and Gal. 4:6.) It did not take long for a Christian thinker to come up with the term "Trinity" to identify this truth of one God in three persons. Theophilus of

Antioch probably used the word around 180. When Emperor Constantine called together church leaders in 325 to settle theological differences that were dividing the faithful, that Council at Nicaea adopted the teaching of this great mystery as a core doctrine of the church.

The use of the masculine term "Father" has been a problem for some faithful Christians. (See question 5.) To provide alternative language, some have invoked "Creator, Redeemer, and Sustainer" as less objectionable terminology. One must be cautious about making these language switches; the meaning of the teaching might unintentionally be altered. For example, "Creator, Redeemer, Sustainer" name three functions of God; the doctrine of the Trinity is not about functions, but about the relationship among three persons. The United Methodist Church calls for the classical language (Father, Son, Holy Spirit) in its baptismal services.

The community of the Trinity represents the fullness of God. This reality was underlined for me when a new Christian said to me that his favorite hymn was the Gloria Patri: "Glory be to the Father and to the Son and to the Holy Ghost; as it was in the beginning, is now, and ever shall be, world without end. Amen." (Many United Methodist congregations sing this act of praise every Sunday.) I had never heard of anyone who preferred this text as a favorite hymn, so I asked, "Why do you choose the Gloria Patri?" "Because," he said, "it tells me more about God than I ever knew before."

> Eternal, Triune God, let all the hosts above,
> let all on earth below record and dwell upon thy love.

Another question: Which person of the Trinity seems closest to you?

 3. What is the practical meaning of belief in the Trinity?

The core teachings of the Christian faith make a difference in how a Christian lives. When a teaching is as complex and mysterious as the doctrine of the Trinity, the connection with "real life," however, may be elusive. What difference does belief in the Trinity make on Monday morning? (For that matter, what difference does it make on Thursday and Friday!)

It helps to remember that this central confession of the triune God came into focus when the early church considered this question: Should Jesus Christ be worshiped? In other words, is Jesus Christ also God? The answer was "Yes," and the church stated the belief that all three persons—Father, Son, and Holy Spirit—are equal in power and in glory. The Father is not better than the Son (there was a false teaching—subordinationism—which claimed that Jesus was subordinate to the Father), and the Holy Spirit is not less than the Son.

It might be a little tough to work the word "subordinationism" into a conversation at the watercooler, but it is important for Christians to understand what it means for the three persons of the Trinity to be equal. There is no one-upmanship in the Trinity, no hierarchy. If we humans are created in the image of God (see question 19), then we are created to reflect that divine equality. When we lift one race above another or give place of privilege to one gender over the other or suggest that youth is preferred to age, we have broken the gift of the Trinity.

The Trinity models relational living for us. The Trinity lives as three persons in community (yet one God). Christians who understand that God's very being is lived in community are called themselves to live in community. It is no accident that the biblical image of the work of God is one of community, a people, corporate life. Our culture values individualism ("I did it my way"), but the biblical truth of the Trinity invites us into a mutual life. Learning to live in community is part of what the church appropriates from the doctrine of God in three persons.

No wonder the Bible underscores that we are members one of another (Eph. 4:25). No wonder the Bible reminds us that "we, who are many, are one body in Christ" (Rom. 12:5). No wonder the Bible instructs us that fellowship with the triune God is to be in a fellowship of love (1 John 1:3; 3:1). If you are not convinced, sneak a look at 1 John 2:10. That is true seven days a week.

> Touched by the lodestone of thy love, let all our hearts agree,
> and ever toward each other move, and ever move toward thee.

Another question: How does life within the church reflect or not reflect the Trinity?

4. Why does God allow suffering?

$\mathcal{A}$ child gets sick with cancer. A huge storm wipes an entire village off the map. A drunken driver speeds into the side of a school bus, killing four, injuring twenty. Accounts of suffering can be picked off the pages of any daily newspaper. Most of the time, we can figure out why the hurt has occurred: human error, bad environmental judgment, spread of disease germs, political shortsightedness. But sometimes there seems to be no rhyme, reason, justification, or jury to explain why suffering has occurred.

Behind both the understandable and the mysteries lies a basic question: Why would a God who is in charge of the world allow such things to happen? United Methodists believe that God created humankind with a capacity for free will (see question 22). That free will has no meaning if our decisions do not have consequences. Our free choice of sin not only breaks our relationship with God, but tears into the fabric of human relationships. Notice in Genesis 3:6–7 that immediately after Adam and Eve—that's our story—sin against God, Adam and Eve also become separated from each other and begin to hide from each other behind fig leaves. Given how scratchy fig leaves are, I'd have to say that they did not make a very good sartorial choice! Their sin against God leads directly to their brokenness from each other. So United Methodists understand that some human suffering is because of what our sin leads us to do to one another.

Even after we make allowances for the sufferings that we humans cause, there remain events and circumstances that seem meaningless and without any reasonable explanation. It turns out that all of creation has fallen from God's will. When God makes things right, it will take both a new heaven and a new earth (Rev. 21:1), made possible because Christ's reconciliation is for all of creation (Col. 1:19–20). God can redeem suffering. The power of the resurrection overcoming Jesus' death on the cross reveals how God can enter into our suffering and bring from it victory.

God creates all to be good (1 Tim. 4:4); God does not cause suffering, but allows it as the companion to human freedom. The good news in this is that God does not leave us alone in our suffering but (as the cross shows) enters fully with us into our times of suffering. And from time to time we get glimpses of that reign of God where the perfect image of God is restored and all creation puts away its groaning and has the full fruit of the Spirit (Rom. 8:18–23). No wonder it is called hope!

> Finish, then, thy new creation; pure and spotless let us be.
> Let us see thy great salvation perfectly restored in thee.

Another question: How is God present with us during times of suffering?

5. Is it OK to call God "Father"?

Let's face it. Human language is going to fall short in any effort to describe or talk about God. God is beyond our verbal capacity! (After all, United Methodists understand that what we know of God is because God has revealed it to us—see question 1.) Even so, the names we use for God become one way we get to know God and one way we introduce others to God.

Names make a difference. What image comes to your mind when you hear the name "Kermit" or "Samantha" or "Luis"? The images that come to your mind and the ones that come to my mind may well be different because we have had different experiences with persons named Kermit, Samantha, and Luis. I'm thinking of Kermit Braswell, Samantha Swivel, and Luis Reinoso. Were you? Probably not. You might have thought of a green frog, a television witch, and a ballplayer. Which of us would be right? (The answer to that question is "yes.")

Biblically, names are so important that often a person's name changes when some major characteristic in his or her life changes (Gen. 17:5; Gen. 17:15; Gen. 32:28; Acts 13:9). Names are not chosen at random (Jer. 33:16; Matt. 1:21).

So then, what name shall we use for God? When Moses asked that exact question, God answered, "I AM WHO I AM." In fact, God said, "This is my name forever" (Exod. 3:13–15). Jesus added to that revelation by referring to God as Father (Matt. 6:9; John 17:1). For centuries, the church has maintained that language and identified the Trinity as Father, Son, and Holy Spirit. The United Methodist Church recognizes that language and calls for its use in the liturgical vocabulary of baptism.

But "I AM" and "Father" do not exhaust the biblical experiences of God. How about the God of Abraham (Exod. 3:15)? How about Shepherd (Ps. 23)? How about Woman in Labor (Isa. 14)? How about Woman in Search of a Coin (Luke 15:8–10)? Creator? Maker? Lord? Jehovah? King? Almighty?

In recent years, United Methodists, among other Christians, have realized that the constant use of only the male images and names for God leads some to think of God as male. 'Tain't so! God is not male; God is spirit (John 4:24). The sole use of "Father" has been a problem for persons for whom "Father" is not a positive term. The same could be said for exclusive use of "Mother" or "Parent" or "King"; there are persons for whom these terms are reminders of bad pasts, even of evil. How is one to be faithful to Scripture and at the same time sensitive to persons for whom traditional language is difficult?

For example, look again at Question 2 for some cautions about casually substituting terms for "Father" in naming the persons of the Trinity. On the other hand, Jesus sets the model for us in using a variety of images and names for God: most frequently Father (John 17:21), God (Matt. 4:4), Lord (Matt. 4:7), Power (Matt. 26:64), Presence (Matt. 12:4); and numerous metaphors: shepherd, woman looking for lost coin, mother hen, waiting father, judge. (This list does not even begin to include names and descriptions of the second and third persons of the Trinity: Truth, Life, Messiah, Advocate, Comforter.)

The very array and range of ways of referring to God reflect the "otherness" of God and our human frailty in trying to talk about and to talk with God.

> 'Tis here we look up and grasp at thy mind,
> 'tis here that we hope thine image to find;
> the means of bestowing thy gifts we embrace;
> but all things are owing to Jesus' grace.

Another question: Which name or image of God means the most to you?

6. What do United Methodists believe about evolution?

United Methodists believe that God is "maker of heaven and earth" (to use the language of two historic creeds, the Apostles' Creed and the Nicene Creed). United Methodists do not agree on how God chose to bring creation into being. Nothing was created without the Word of God (John 1:3). All things were created through Christ and for Christ (Col. 1:16). The Bible is clear that creation is the work of God.

But the question remains: How did God go about creating? Many United Methodists believe that "how" questions are beyond the revelation of Scripture. The Scriptures contain all that is necessary for salvation (as stated in the Articles of Religion and the Confession of Faith—see question 49), but not all that is necessary for the study of geography, history, and science. The accounts in Genesis make clear that God is Creator; humankind and the rest of the created order are creature. The creative activity of God gives meaning to the development of life.

Most (but not all) scientists accept the theory of evolution. Nothing in that theory denies the formation of the world by God. In fact, the theory of evolution leaves unanswered the very questions the Scripture addresses: Who? Why? Where from here?

The tensions between science and faith emerge most severely when each tries to answer questions intended for the other. Ask me how to play dartball; ask my wife, Toni, how to grow houseplants; but don't ask her to describe the intricacies of throwing a dart at the small square for a triple, and don't ask me whether trimming a Christmas cactus will cause it to grow or to die. Toni and I don't do well handling each other's questions; neither do science and faith.

Most United Methodists—I say this with great authority because, after all, I asked three people!—make their decision about evolution based on their acceptance (or not) of its scientific validity. God called things into existence that did not exist (Rom. 4:17). Life exists within God (John 5:26). God spoke and creation began (Gen. 1:1–3). Whether the account be in the images and language of biblical writers drawing on their own reference points or whether the account be spelled out in complex terms of DNA and genetic selection and molecular structure, the bottom line is the same: this is the work of God.

> God, in whom they move and live, let every creature sing,
> glory to their Maker give, and homage to their King.

Another question: Why is evolution such a "hot button" issue for many Christians?

2

Jesus Christ

 7. What does "incarnation" mean?

Right now on my favorite baseball team, the St. Louis Cardinals, there is a player named Juan Encarnación. I love the way that name rolls off the tongue. His last name is in Spanish the word that in English is Incarnation. The literal translation of his name is "embodiment." There is some burden in carrying such a name! Embodying what? Embodying family values? Embodying good baseball practices? Embodying success?

Christians (including United Methodists) proclaim that Jesus is the Incarnation, the *Encarnación*. What does Jesus embody? John 1:14 names the answer: the Word. That is, what God had to say, what God wanted to express, what God wished to reveal was made flesh in Jesus. "The Word became flesh and lived among us."

That is strong talk. Claiming that a man in Palestine about two thousand years ago was fully human (flesh) and fully divine (Word) is a central affirmation of Christian faith. Divine, maybe. Human, probably. But both? Yet centuries of Christians have made precisely that proclamation: Jesus of Nazareth is God incarnate.

The humanity of Jesus was real. Hebrews 4:15 notes that Jesus underwent the same temptations that we do. He got hungry and ate (Matt. 9:10). His death was real, not pretend (Luke 23:46). He took on our humanity in order to redeem us (Rom. 8:3–4). He bore our sins in his death on the cross (Rom. 5:8). His resurrection offers us new life (Rom. 8:11).

The divinity of Jesus was real. John 1:1 begins with a clear statement that this Word that became flesh was God. Colossians 1:19 is a poetic statement of "the fullness of God" dwelling in Jesus Christ. Philippians 2:6 is a reminder that Christ Jesus was "in the form of God." There is no separation from God's love in Christ Jesus (Rom. 8:38–39).

Incarnation, then, means that the Divine One and the Human One are mysteriously the same. The Nicene Creed shouts of this gift: "God from God, Light from Light, true God from true God"! In Jesus Christ, there is full humanity and full divinity.

From time to time, some Christians have struggled so much with this belief that they have tried to carve away some of it. Docetists argued that Jesus only seemed to be human. Modalists claimed no distinctive work for Jesus, the Son, to do. Subordinationalists (now there is a great word to show your friends how much you have learned) said that the Son was less God than the Father. Monarchianists insisted that God the Son was not equal to God the Father. Each time the church has heard these testing claims, the church has found again the biblical understanding that Jesus came as both fully human and fully divine. Incarnation.

> Veiled in flesh the Godhead see; hail th'incarnate Deity,
> pleased with us in flesh to dwell, Jesus, our Emmanuel.

Another question: What are the gifts of Christ's humanity? of Christ's divinity?

 ## 8. Was Jesus really born of a virgin?

Almost every United Methodist would assert that he or she believes in the virgin birth of Jesus, but what individuals mean by that affirmation varies widely. For some, the virgin birth means that Mary, the mother of Jesus, did not have sexual intercourse before the conception of Jesus in her womb ("conceived by the Holy Spirit," as the Apostles' Creed says). (Maybe the better term would be "virgin conception.") A few persons, perhaps pleased that they have learned to pronounce the word, declare the birth of Jesus to be "parthenogenesis," a scientific term used to describe births in nature that do occur without male input. Other United Methodists understand that "virgin birth" is the symbol chosen by the church to underscore the fact that God (the Holy Spirit) was part and parcel of what happens in the birth of the Messiah.

Matthew 1:18–25 and Luke 1:26–34 and John 1:13 all point toward a straightforward interpretation that Mary was a virgin and Jesus was conceived not by human sexual relations but by the intervention of the Holy Spirit. On the other hand, Mark, who prepared a shorter "heart of the matter" Gospel record, makes no mention of such a miracle. Paul explores many angles of Christology (teachings about Christ) and makes no reference to a virgin birth. Either Mark and Paul just assumed it, or they did not find the whole matter of much importance.

Some translations of Isaiah 7:14 say that "a virgin shall conceive, and bear a son." Does this point toward a literal understanding of the virgin birth? Recent studies have shown that the word sometimes rendered "virgin" in Isaiah 7:14 actually is a word that means "young woman of marriageable age." Such examination of the Isaiah text leaves unanswered the question of an Old Testament prophecy.

Early Christians would not have thought that the virgin birth of Jesus made him unique. The Greek and Roman cultures were filled with stories of gods who were born of virgins: Perseus, Dionysius, Horus, and Mithra, for example. The statement of Jesus' virgin birth seems to be a clear celebration that our Lord is both human and divine.

Some scholars have argued that when the ancient creeds spoke of the virgin birth, the emphasis was not on "virgin" but was on "birth." At issue was whether or not Jesus was human. "Yes!" they taught. "He was born, a human being!" Classic United Methodist documents (see question 49) take for granted that Jesus was born of a virgin. Contemporary United Methodists disagree on whether "virgin birth" is a biological statement or a theological statement.

> Christ, by highest heaven adored; Christ, the everlasting Lord;
> late in time behold him come, offspring of a virgin's womb.

Another question: To what extent is the doctrine of the virgin birth essential to salvation?

9. Where was Jesus when the world was created?

There has never been a time when Jesus Christ did not exist.

Having said that, let us back up a bit and come at this question from another side. Hang with me for a moment! For Christians, a heresy is a religious doctrine or teaching that is contrary to the church's accepted truth. For United Methodists (and most other Christians), that means that a heresy is an error that departs from biblical revelation.

Now jump back to the fourth century. A church leader named Arius taught that within the Trinity, the Son was created by the Father (and thus was a creature). In an official theological decision, the church said this view was a heresy, a false teaching. (It was called "Arianism." How would you like to have a heresy named after you?)

What difference does all this make? Arianism collapses one of the chief tenets of the doctrine of the Trinity, that Father, Son, and Holy Spirit are eternal. (If the Son were created by the Father, the Son would not be eternal. This will all make more sense if you sleep tonight with the answer to Question 2 under your pillow.) The biblical truth is that the Son is fully divine, so there has never been a time when the Son did not exist.

In a comment on John 1:1, John Wesley wrote that "the Word existed without any beginning." This reality is called the preexistence of Christ. The biblical support for this is found in Colossians 1:15–20 ("He himself is before all things"); Hebrews 1:1–3 ("the exact imprint of God's very being"); John 1:1 ("In the beginning was the Word, . . . and the Word was God"; and Philippians 2:5–8 ("in the form of God").

The Articles of Religion of The Methodist Church use the term "everlasting" and "maker . . . of all things" to refer to all three persons of the Trinity. The Confession of Faith of the Evangelical United Brethren Church uses "eternal" and "Creator" to speak of the Trinity. (Look at Question 49 for thoughts about the authority of the Articles and the Confession.) So we come back to where we began: "There has never been a time when Jesus Christ did not exist."

O Love divine, what hast thou done! The immortal God hath died for
   me!
The Father's coeternal Son bore all my sins upon the tree.
Th'immortal God for me hath died: My Lord, my Love, is crucified!

Another question: Because Christ was present at creation, what do
we know about the nature of creation?

10. Why did Jesus have to die?

Jesus said he did not have to die. In John 10:18, our Lord affirms
that he lays down his life of his own accord, not because he is forced
to do so. But Jesus also says that, even though he did not have to do
so, he would lay down his life in order for persons to be ransomed
(Mark 10:45). The early church understood that this plan for salvation was God's intent all along (Acts 2:23; Matt. 26:56).

United Methodists agree with most Christians who assert that the
death of Jesus made things right between God and humankind. This
action is sometimes called "the atonement." The word "atonement"
means making into a restored relationship two entities that have
been broken apart—"at-one-ment." What was broken apart? God
and humankind. Our choice of sin broke us from the holy God. How
are we reunited with God? First Thessalonians 5:9–10 is one way
Paul declared that the death of Jesus restored us sinners to life: "Our
Lord Jesus Christ . . . died for us, so . . . we may live with him."

There are several theories of the atonement, and United
Methodists vary in the emphasis they put on these concepts. (1) One
view is that we sinners were owned by evil (the devil), and a ransom
had to be paid in order to win us back to God (1 Tim. 2:6). Jesus'
death is that ransom payment in our behalf. (2) Another understanding is that God's anger at sin could be assuaged only by a sacrifice (Rom. 5:18). No sinful human could make that sacrifice, so
sinless Jesus became our substitute and took all God's anger on himself. (3) A third stress argues that the atonement is simply the moral
influence of love, which is seen most fully in the death of Jesus on
the cross (1 Pet. 2:21). Humankind is moved by this love to accept
God's gracious salvation. (4) Another interpretation is that Jesus'
death on the cross showed the power of evil, but that the resurrec-

tion showed the ultimate victory of God (Col. 2:15). Without the death of Jesus, there is no victory in the resurrection.

There is some thread of biblical truth in each of these perceptions. In each case, United Methodists recognize that the death of Christ on the cross was sufficient for our salvation. (The Articles of Religion of The Methodist Church call it "perfect redemption.") The sum is that Jesus died in order for us to be saved.

'Tis mystery all: th'Immortal dies! Who can explore his strange design?
In vain the first-born seraph tries to sound the depths of love divine.
'Tis mercy all! Let earth adore; let angel minds inquire no more.

Another question: Which theory of the atonement brings the most light to your Christian journey?

11. What is the meaning of the resurrection of Jesus?

There is no report of anyone who saw Jesus rise from the dead, yet the truth of his resurrection is the heart of the Christian faith. Jesus' resurrection is so central that Paul says that without that resurrection we are still perishing in our sins, and our faith is futile (1 Cor. 15:12–20).

The early believers expressed their confidence in the resurrection by relaying accounts of appearance by the risen Christ: for example, to the women at the newly emptied tomb (Matt. 28:9), to two disciples who were out walking (Mark 16:12), to the eleven disciples (Mark 16:14), to Thomas (John 20:26), to seven of the disciples who were fishing (John 21:4–7). Paul also claimed a vision of the risen Lord (Acts 9:5) and listed others to whom Jesus appeared (1 Cor. 15:5–8).

The resurrection of Jesus has meaning only if Jesus was really dead. From time to time, naysayers have proposed that Jesus only appeared to be dead. (Although the lily is often used as an Easter symbol of resurrection, perhaps it is only a partial sign of the resurrection, because the lily only appears to be dead—there is actually life within the dormant bulb.) Jesus was dead. If he were not, the resurrection is a hoax and faith is a fraud.

The evidence of the resurrection is the transformation of those who encountered the risen Christ. Who would not be transformed by meeting the risen Lord! And because he is alive, we of the twenty-first century can also meet him. Resurrection is not the same as resuscitation; if someone is resuscitated, he or she will still end up on the obituary page in time; Jesus, who was resurrected, is still alive.

If Jesus is alive, why isn't he walking around on earth where folks can see him? The teaching of the church is that Jesus ascended in a cloud (Acts 1:9). In the Bible, the presence of a cloud is often the sign of God's presence (see Exod. 13:21 and Luke 9:35, for example). Whatever happened in that scene, there is the assurance that God was present. United Methodists celebrate that each year on the fortieth day after Easter (or on the following Sunday), Ascension Day. The humanity of Jesus has ascended into heaven, where Jesus will reign (1 Cor. 15:25). Even so, the liturgy of Holy Communion proclaims, "The risen Christ is with us!"

The resurrection of Jesus Christ gives us the hope of our own resurrection into eternal life (1 Pet. 1:3–4). The resurrection of Jesus Christ equips believers to walk in newness of life even now (Rom. 6:5). The resurrection of Jesus Christ can move us from sin to justification (Rom. 4:24–25). The resurrection of Jesus Christ is the first fruit of the community of everlasting life (2 Cor. 4:14). Where I come from, that sounds like good news.

> Love's redeeming work is done, . . . Fought the fight, the battle won, . . .
> Death in vain forbids him rise, . . . Christ has opened paradise, Alleluia!

Another question: What does the resurrection of Christ mean for your daily life?

12. Will Jesus come again?

Yes.

United Methodists are not likely to get into extended debate about when Jesus will return. On the other hand, some traditions argue extensively about a thousand-year period of suffering or a thousand-year of rule, or a period of tribulation, or . . . well, most any way of pinning down what God has in mind for the future. Occasionally, believers will work out a complicated formula that seems to name the exact time—and perhaps even place—of the return of Jesus. Needless to say, so far these predictions have all been wrong. Jesus cautioned against such guesswork (Matt. 24:36; Acts 1:7).

At the end of *Explanatory Notes upon the New Testament*, John Wesley attached something of a timeline for the events leading toward the return of Christ. After conjecturing some dates, he closes that flow with the general word "afterward." Mr. Wesley recognized the danger of getting too specific with descriptions of God's ultimate actions. Students of the Bible use the term "eschatology" to identify those matters dealing with "last things." Although some Christians spend a great deal of spiritual energy on the "rapture" as the fullest expression of Christ's return, United Methodists typically do not. ("Rapture" is based on 1 Thess. 4:13–18; Paul is offering encouragement to the Thessalonians by teaching that the whole family of God, both dead and alive, will belong to Christ.)

Some persons feel that it is inappropriate to speak of the "second coming" of Christ, because that language implies that Christ is not present with us now. An alternative term is "final coming" or "Parousia," a Greek word meaning "presence" or "arrival." The Articles of Religion and the Confession of Faith (as well as traditional creeds such as the Apostles' Creed and the Nicene Creed) all make claim on the triumphant return of Jesus. After all the debate and discussion, the chief point is that God is going to win and that Jesus Christ is evidence of that victory.

Part of the United Methodist understanding of the Parousia is an expectation that Christ will come as judge. In his *Sermons,* John Wesley says that each of our thoughts, every one of our words, and all our deeds will be subject to the examination of God. No wonder that we rejoice that our salvation (see questions 25–30) is by faith given to us by grace and (praise the Lord!) not by our final day's report card.

Lo, he comes with clouds descending, once for favored sinners slain; thousand, thousand saints attending swell the triumph of his train. Hallelujah! Hallelujah! Hallelujah! God appears on earth to reign.

Another question: How is your life today affected by the promise of Christ's final return?

3

Holy Spirit

 13. What does the Holy Spirit have to do with Jesus?

The Holy Spirit is a coequal, coeternal member of the Trinity (see question 2). In the first centuries of the life of the church, much of the debate and clarification was about Christology: Who is Jesus Christ? As the church began to express the faith in creedal form (around the fourth century), the doctrine of the full divinity of the Holy Spirit moved to center stage.

The Old Testament uses the Hebrew word *ruah* for the Spirit; that word means "breath." The New Testament uses the Greek word *pneuma* for the Spirit; that word means "wind." These root words remind us that the Holy Spirit is as essential as breathing and the Holy Spirit moves as freely as the breezes (John 3:8). The Spirit moved over the waters as creation broke into being (Gen. 1:2). The Spirit distributes spiritual gifts as the Spirit chooses (1 Cor. 12:11). The Spirit intercedes for us when our prayers are fragile (Rom. 8:26–27).

Jesus promises that the Holy Spirit will come when the disciples are no longer able to see Jesus (John 14:16). In this verse, the word chosen by our Lord to depict the Holy Spirit is usually translated "Advocate" or "Helper" or "Intercessor." In Greek, the word is *paraclete*. Just as "paralegal" defines someone who works alongside an attorney and "paradox" means two truths that are alongside each other, so the word *paraclete* means "someone who is called alongside." That's the Holy Spirit!

Jesus says that he will ask the Father to send the Holy Spirit (John 14:16), and in some sense the story of the New Testament is the story of the coming of the Holy Spirit. Acts 2:1–12 breaks open the appearance of the Holy Spirit at Pentecost. The power of the Spirit in Christian lives is of the essence; 1 Corinthians 12:3 says that "no one can say 'Jesus is Lord' except by the Holy Spirit."

Around the year 600, there was a major dispute in the church as to whether the Holy Spirit proceeded from just the Father or from the Father and the Son. United Methodism is in the journey of those who argue that the Spirit proceeds from the Father and the Son. The Greek term *filioque,* which means "and from the Son," is used to make this distinction. Few persons today get very exercised about this doctrinal fine point, but it is a helpful reminder of the Spirit, who is the Spirit of Christ (Rom. 8:9; Gal. 4:6; Phil. 1:19).

> No one can truly say that Jesus is the Lord,
> unless thou take the veil away and breathe the living Word.

Another question: When is the Holy Spirit most real to you?

14. What is the Holy Spirit's work within the church?

United Methodists pray frequently for the Holy Spirit to impact the Christian journey.

For example, after persons are baptized in the name of the Father and of the Son and of the Holy Spirit, the pastor says to each one just baptized: "The Holy Spirit work within you, that being born through water and the Spirit, you may be a faithful disciple of Jesus Christ" (*BOW,* p. 91).

For example, in part of the prayer of Great Thanksgiving in the Communion service, the pastor prays, "Pour out your Holy Spirit on us gathered here, and on these gifts of bread and wine. . . . By your Spirit make us one with Christ, . . . showing forth the fruit of the Spirit" (*BOW,* p. 69).

For example, in the service for confirmation and profession of faith, the pastor asks that "the Spirit confirm you in the faith and fellowship of all true disciples of Jesus Christ" (*BOW,* p. 108).

For example, in the service of ordination of an elder, the bishop prays, "Lord, pour upon [this person] the Holy Spirit for the office and work of an elder, in the name of the Father, and of the Son, and of the Holy Spirit" (*BOW,* p. 677).

For example, in the dismissal at a service of death and resurrection, the pastor asks a blessing that God "grant you to be strengthened with might through God's Spirit in your inner being" (*BOW*, p. 151).

The Holy Spirit gives us the gift of faith (1 Cor. 12:3). The Holy Spirit equips us with gifts for the journey of faith (1 Cor. 12:4–6). The Holy Spirit moves us toward holy living, sanctification (2 Thess. 2:13). The Holy Spirit works to give unity to the church (Eph. 4:3–4). The Holy Spirit gives us hope for a good tomorrow (Rom. 8:16–17). The Holy Spirit even kicks our prayers up a notch! (Rom. 8:26–27).

One emphasis in United Methodist theology is a belief that the Holy Spirit gives the gift of assurance (Rom. 8:16). John Wesley said that the teaching of assurance was "one grand part of the testimony which God has given [the Methodists] to bear to all humankind" (*Works*, vol. 1, p. 285). United Methodists understand that normally a person who has been saved through faith is also given assurance of that salvation. United Methodists love to tell the story (already quoted once in this book!) of May 24, 1738, when Mr. Wesley himself gained this gift of assurance at a meeting at Aldersgate Street in London, where he reports, "I felt my heart strangely warmed. I felt I did trust in Christ, Christ alone for salvation; and an assurance was given me that He had taken away my sins, even mine, and saved me from the law of sin and death." This assurance is a gift of the Holy Spirit.

> God, through the Spirit we shall know if thou within us shine,
> and sound, with all thy saints below, the depths of love divine.

Another question: How has the Holy Spirit given you the gift of assurance?

15. What is the Holy Spirit's work outside the church?

Jacob Albright was the founder of the Evangelical Church (which became part of the Evangelical United Brethren Church in 1946 and part of The United Methodist Church in 1968). As a layperson, he was known as "an honest tile maker." What is striking about this description is how it illustrates some of the roots of a United Methodist understanding that holy living is not just about "getting it right at church," but is also about following the Spirit's lead in daily life. Jacob Albright thought the Holy Spirit wanted the tiles Albright made to be of the best clay, the best kiln work, and the best quality possible. And the Holy Spirit wanted him to tell the truth about the product. United Methodists recognize that the Holy Spirit works outside the church.

The Holy Spirit will blow where the Spirit chooses (John 3:8). This means that not only does the Holy Spirit hear and respond to our prayers, but the Holy Spirit also goes ahead of us. The Holy Spirit is already at work in the world beyond the church. What kind of things does the Holy Spirit do in the world? Jesus named a few: be among the poor, help persons come out of bondage to those things that would limit them, open the eyes of those who cannot see; help oppressed people become free; and let people know that God is still in charge (Luke 4:18–19).

Believing that the Holy Spirit precedes us to places of need (see question 25 on prevenient grace), United Methodists seek to find those places where God is already at work and then move to join God in that work. John Wesley was so sure that the Spirit was active in meeting the world's needs that he said that being among the poor, working with the poor, and learning from the poor were means of receiving God's grace. No wonder United Methodists get engaged in social justice and disaster relief and legislative battles and eradication of racism and fights for human fulfillment—these are places where God's grace is to be found!

Peace and justice and health and nurture are God's intent for all persons (Isa. 61:1–4). Wherever God is moving toward the sanctification of society, United Methodists tend to take that work in the world seriously. Sometimes we disagree about what is and what is not God's movement, but even if we are not of one mind as to where God is at work, seldom do we disagree about the importance of finding out.

> Forth in thy name, O Lord, I go, my daily labor to pursue;
> thee, only thee, resolved to know in all I think or speak or do.

Another question: Where is the Holy Spirit at work beyond the church in your community?

16. What is the unforgivable sin against the Holy Spirit?

Sometimes when I am reading the Bible I wish I had an eraser at hand. There are some texts that make me so uncomfortable that I simply wish they were not there. Matthew 12:31–32 (and companion verses in Mark 3:28–29 and Luke 12:10) is such a place. There is little space in which to hide from these verses; in the Bible I am looking at now, they are printed in red: something Jesus himself said.

What are we to make of this statement, that even though sin and blasphemy will be forgiven (even blaspheming the Son of Man—Matt. 12:32), sin against the Holy Spirit will not be forgiven? What is this unforgivable sin?

John Wesley (in his *Explanatory Notes*) wrote about the text: "How much stir has been made about this! . . . And yet there is nothing plainer in all the Bible." The heart of the matter is a refusal to believe the gospel. In this passage, Matthew (and Mark and Luke also) is reporting on Pharisees who gave the devil credit for the good works done by Jesus (Matt. 12:24; Mark 3:22; Luke 11:15). To identify God as Satan makes repentance impossible. To give evil credit for what God has done is to miss the God whose love comes toward us. For some persons, these passages create great anxiety. If you are worrying about it, it is a pretty good sign that you are not guilty of this sin! God is not "out to get you." (Note the expansive nature of God's forgiveness—"every sin and blasphemy.")

All moral value is turned upside down when credit for the work of the Holy Spirit is given to Beelzebul, the ruler of demons (Matt. 12:27). This is Jesus' condemnation of the Pharisees, who were trying to trick him (Luke 11:54), and not some overarching development of a list of sins from which there is no recovery. "Pharisees!" Jesus is saying. "These miracles are the work of the Holy Spirit through me; if you think otherwise, you have missed seeing God."

If taken in the larger view of these verses, this shocking passage is actually a word of grace and encouragement. The reign of God is breaking into our world (Matt. 12:22—the healing of the demoniac—is a sign of how God wants the world to be). There is forgiveness for sin! There is even forgiveness for blasphemy (Mark 3:28)!

The Holy Spirit will teach us for times of trial (Luke 12:12). There is a lot of good news here for those who will see the Spirit at work!

Sinners, turn: why will you die? God, the Spirit, asks you why;
he, who all your lives hath strove, wooed you to embrace his love.

Another question: What would you say to someone who thinks she or he has committed the sin against the Holy Spirit?

 17. What role does speaking in tongues have in United Methodism?

On the one hand, a United Methodist friend told me that from time to time his prayer time emerges in a language he does not understand. There is, he says, such an ecstasy of joy and release in such praying that he delights when that gift is given to him. It is not, he tells me, something that can be called up on demand. It always comes as a gift of the Spirit.

On the other hand, another United Methodist friend has said he can create the sound of speaking in tongues simply by rapidly repeating the words "I tie my bow tie; I tie my bow tie; my bow tie I tie." (My guess is that you just tried saying that!) His joke is a mild rebuke to those who give emphasis to praying in tongues.

On the question of speaking in tongues, United Methodists are a mixed bag! It would have to be noted, however, that in United Methodist settings public glossolalia (from the Greek word for "tongue") is rare, and private devotional glossolalia is infrequently noted. (For example, in fifty years of attending United Methodist annual conferences, I can recall only two occasions of an individual speaking in tongues. One wonders: how many hesitate to report their personal prayer experience for fear of ridicule?)

Some persons see biblical roots for glossolalia in the Pentecost story in Acts 2:1–13. The languages spoken there were not unknown, indistinguishable speaking that needed interpretation. This Pentecost story is quite the opposite; persons understood quite well what was being said "in the native language of each" (Acts 2:6). The remarkable thing is that those who spoke so clearly in these varieties of language were not people who were trained in those languages. Pentecost is not about hidden truth; it is about revealed truth, God gate-crashing our human expectations in order to communicate with all people.

The apostle Paul viewed glossolalia as chiefly a personal spiritual gift, not necessarily intended to enrich the whole church (1 Cor. 14:2–5). In fact, Paul asserts that interpretation will be needed if the tongues are to build up the church. It was not a gift for everyone, any more than healing or leadership or teaching were gifts for everyone (1 Cor. 12:28–31). Paul's caution is that there is a gift that surpasses all these gifts from the Spirit: love. (The famous thirteenth chapter of 1 Corinthians—"the love chapter"—follows the admonition to seek the greatest gift.)

Some Pentecostal traditions have split off from what is now United Methodism because some persons felt the predecessor bodies of The United Methodist Church downplayed (or even were hostile to) the gift of speaking in tongues. Both the Articles of Religion (of The Methodist Church) and the Confession of Faith (of the Evangelical United Brethren Church) pronounce clearly that public worship should be in a language understood by the people. Even though that injunction grew chiefly out of a concern about the use of Latin in Roman Catholic worship, it does reflect a vigilant care that experiences of worship unite rather than divide us.

O Thou who camest from above, the pure celestial fire to impart,
kindle a flame of sacred love upon the mean altar of my heart.

Another question: What experiences have you had with speaking in tongues?

18. What are the gifts of the Spirit?

The gifts of God are many. Every time Paul starts to make a list, he gets on a roll. How about 1 Corinthians 12? Wisdom, knowledge, faith, healing, miracles, prophecy, discernment, tongues, interpretation. Each awareness of a spiritual gift makes Paul think of another!

How about Romans 12? Prophecy, ministry, teaching, exhorting, giving, leading, showing compassion. I bet Paul had particular persons in mind as he unfolded this list.

How about Ephesians 4? Apostles, prophets, evangelists, pastors, teachers. Not everyone has these gifts; only some are gifted to be evangelists, for example.

In each case, the gift is a gift of the Spirit. United Methodists ask about those who seek to become clergy: Do they "give evidence of God's gifts for ordained ministry, evidence of God's grace in their lives, and promise of future usefulness in the mission of the Church"? (*BOD*, ¶304.1f). Persons received into professing membership in The United Methodist Church promise, among other things, to participate in the ministries of the church with their gifts. Two dimensions emerge from these inquiries and promises: (1) the gift is the work of the Spirit in this person's life and (2) these spiritual gifts (for clergy or for lay) are never about the individual; the gifts are given for the work of the whole family of God (Rom. 12:3–5; 1 Cor. 12:14–26).

Local churches often use spiritual gift inventories to help persons discover how God has gifted them for the benefit of the work of the whole church. Persons who have been in study and accountability groups often get the counsel of companions about gifts for ministry. It is not always easy to hear from trusted colleagues that I have an unused gift that God has tried to give me! Paul had to tell Timothy twice (1 Tim. 4:14 and 2 Tim. 1:6) to keep alive the gift that had been recognized, confirmed, and authorized by the laying on of hands. (Laying on of hands is a New Testament practice continued today to mark the pouring out of the Holy Spirit for gifts in ministry.)

Those gifts of the Spirit bear good fruit: love, joy, peace, patience, kindness, generosity, faithfulness, gentleness, and self-control (Gal. 5:22–23). When United Methodists are at their best—and that is not always!—the gifts of the Holy Spirit are used without personal pride or privilege, and the fruit of the Spirit abounds wherever life is touched by the Spirit's guidance.

Sometimes I tell a church council that if all its decisions make as much sense at the neighborhood store as they do at church, then probably some of the decisions are wrong. The church does not decide in the same way the world does. As Paul wrote the church at Galatia: "If we live by the Spirit, let us also be guided by the Spirit" (Gal. 5:25).

> The gift which he on one bestows, we all delight to prove,
> the grace through every vessel flows in purest streams of love.

Another question: What spiritual gifts do others say that you have?

4

Humanity

 19. What does it mean to say that people are created in the image of God?

(1) Genesis 1:26 indicates that God created humankind in God's own image so that humans have dominion over the rest of the created order. First, being in the image of God means responsibility as stewards of creation.

(2) Genesis 1:27 spells out that when God created humankind in God's image, God created them as male and female. Second, being created in the image of God means that we are created for relationships.

(3) Genesis 1:26 says that God created humankind to be in God's likeness, to live in the moral life of God. Third, being created in the image of God means that we are intended to be in relationship with God and God's values.

John Wesley (in his sermon on "The New Birth") used three phrases to mark these dimensions of being created in the image of God: (a) natural image—we are a spiritual being with freedom of will; (b) political image—we are governor of the created world and engaged in relationship with others; and (c) moral image—we are intended for holiness and righteousness (*Works,* vol 2, p. 188).

As we shall explore in questions 20 and 21, this perfect image, this unbroken reflection of God, was shattered by human sin. (It took the perfection of Jesus Christ to restore the image.)

To be in the image of God is not to be God. To be in the image of God is to be free to obey God. United Methodists take with great seriousness all three implications of being in God's image: (a) natural image—we invite persons to be in relationship with God;

(b) political image—we invite persons to care for the environment and to care for personal relationships; (c) moral image—we invite persons to live lives of personal and social holiness.

All persons are created in the image of God, even those we do not like, those we do not respect, and those whom we actually fear. (And that image is broken in all humankind, including those whom we enjoy, those whom we honor, and those who are "on our side.")

Do United Methodists always live in perfect reflection of God's love, God's justice, God's image? No, of course not. Not even close. But the God who created humankind in God's image is still at work to restore us all to that image.

> Maker, in whom we live, in whom we are and move,
> the glory, power, and praise receive for thy creating love.

Another question: What of God's intention do you see in people you know?

 2〇. Are people good or bad?

God is love and God creates only good. John Wesley wrote, "Accordingly, [humankind] at [their] creation was full of love. . . . God is full of justice, mercy, and truth; so was [humankind] as [they] came from the hands of [their] Creator; God is spotless purity; and so [humankind] was in the beginning pure from every sinful blot" (*Works,* vol. 2, p. 188). God created humankind good; theologians call that "original righteousness." In fact, Genesis 1:31 reports that "God saw everything that he had made, and indeed, it was very good."

But, there is an "oops"! Given freedom, humankind made choices that caused a fall from the goodness of God's creation; Genesis 3:1–7 tells how that happened with Adam and Eve—the forbidden fruit thing. (Remember that "Adam" is Hebrew for "human being" and "Eve" is Hebrew for "life giver," so the stories of Adam and Eve are in truth the reality for all people.) Evil becomes part of the human picture.

A bit of anonymous verse sums up the situation.

> God's plan made a hopeful beginning,
> But we spoiled our chances by sinning.
>   We trust that the story
>   Will end in God's glory,
> But at present the other side's winning.

The answer to the question "Are people good or bad" seems to be "Both." Creation: good. Fall: bad. And God is at work to restore humankind to righteousness. As Ephesians 4:24 states it: "Clothe yourselves with the new self, created according to the likeness of God in true righteousness and holiness."

Just as the goodness in which humankind was created was total ("God saw everything that he had made, and indeed, it was very good"), so the fall into sin was also total. Not only is everyone in bondage to sin (1 John 1:8; John 8:7), but everything about everyone is in that bondage (Rom. 7:14–20).

This brokenness from God's will can take individual, personal form and can take social, institutional form. But the good news is that God's grace is already at work to bring humankind back into goodness. God's prevenient (or common) grace is at work (see question 25) so that good things do happen, even from less than good people; good things do happen, even from less than good societies. Such glimpses of goodness make it so that we can live and function even while in bondage to sin, as we taste the firstfruits of the gifts of the Spirit. "We know that the whole creation has been groaning in labor pains until now; and not only the creation, but we ourselves, who have the first fruits of the Spirit, groan inwardly while we wait for adoption, the redemption of our bodies" (Rom. 8:22–23).

> I have long withstood his grace, long provoked him to his face,
> would not hearken to his calls, grieved him by a thousand falls.

Another question: Why would God allow sin to come into God's good creation?

21. What is original sin?

In our culture, we give a lot of attention to persons who are first to do something: our first president, George Washington; the first person on the moon, Neil Armstrong; the first child born to English parents in America, Virginia Dare; the first professional basketball player to score 100 points in a single game, Wilt Chamberlain; the first man to run a mile in less than four minutes, Roger Bannister; the first person to install an electric traffic light, Lester Wire. (I just threw in that last one because I love the appropriateness of his name!)

We admire firsts. We appreciate originality, so perhaps we are intrigued by the possibility of being involved with *original* sin. Sorry. Research shows that 99.99999 percent of sins have already been committed by someone else. You are more likely to win the lottery fourteen straight times than you are to commit a brand-new sin. (Research also shows that 92.6 percent of statistics are made up on the spot!) No matter what your favorite sin might be, someone else has already done it!

Original sin is not about being the first; it is about sin being in our origins. It is part of the package of being human. It is what article VII of The Methodist Church's Articles of Religion calls "the corruption of the nature of every man" and what article VII of the Evangelical United Brethren Church's Confession of Faith notes as "man . . . inclined to evil." This original sin leads to actual sins for which each is held responsible.

Unlike the tradition of Augustine (a fourth- and fifth-century theologian), United Methodists do not teach that it is the sexual act that passes on the infection of sin. Romans 5:12–21 and 1 Corinthians 15:22 reveal that our sinful nature is in our human origin (Adam). No one escapes the affliction of original sin (Rom. 3:10). (Wesley contrasted original sin with actual sins: actual sins are willful transgression of God's law as we best know it.)

Only Christ can release us from bondage to original sin. The Articles of Religion teach that "we are accounted righteous before God only for the merit of our Lord and Saviour Jesus Christ." The harvest of original sin is death ("all die in Adam," 1 Cor. 15:22). Jesus Christ is life (John 11:25). Philip William Otterbein, one of the saints in the roots of United Methodism, once preached a sermon entitled "The Salvation-bringing Incarnation and Glorious Victory of Jesus Christ over the Devil and Death." (Perhaps catchy sermon titles were not important in the eighteenth century!) In that sermon, Dr. Otterbein said, "All of us lie under this death since the fall." But then the preacher pointed to Romans 8:1: "There is therefore now no condemnation for those who are in Christ Jesus."

> O come and dwell in me, Spirit of power within,
> and bring the glorious liberty from sorrow, fear, and sin.

Another question: How would you explain original sin to a six-year-old child?

22. Do people have free will?

John Wesley and Charles Wesley, two brothers central to the emergence of the Methodist movement, did what brothers often do: they argued. Organization and preaching were often the tools used by John; music and hymns were often the tools used by Charles. (He wrote over six thousand hymns.) Once they had a debate about a hymn written by Charles. John even refused to include the offending stanza in hymnals he edited.

What caused this fuss? In the hymn "Love Divine, All Loves Excelling," Charles had written "Take away our *power* of sinning" (emphasis added). John hit the theological ceiling. He disputed the choice of words: in effect, he said, "If we have no *power* to sin, there is no meaning to our obedience." John won that fight; when United Methodists intone that hymn today, they sing, "Take away our *bent* to sinning." (Other hymnals, such as Lutheran and Presbyterian, choose to sing, "Take away our *love* of sinning." The British Methodists' hymnbook and the Episcopal hymnal stick with John Wesley's original solution and omit the stanza entirely!)

What difference does it make? United Methodists are in the tradition of Jacob Arminius, who insisted that God's grace is universally available. (This view is over against a strict insight by some who followed John Calvin; they claimed that God's sovereignty meant that God chose—predestined—those to be saved; some even said that the implication of that understanding was that God also chose those who would be damned.) The implication of Arminianism (which is what the teachings of Dr. Arminius are called) is that as a result of this universal grace all human beings have free will to choose whether or not to accept Christ.

The Articles of Religion (article VIII) and the Confession of Faith (article VII) are transparent in insisting that this free will is not a natural thing for humans; it is available only because of the grace of God. But it is a grace given to all persons (John 1:9). United Methodism rejects any view of Christ's saving gifts that does not make those gifts available to all persons. Free will—another gift of God—makes it possible for each one to "choose this day whom you will serve" (Josh. 24:15).

The United Methodist teaching about free will is a companion to the teaching about the universal atonement. If salvation in Christ is not available to all persons, then the atonement is limited. United Methodists would not draw that box around the atonement (see question 10). God gives each person the freedom to accept or deny that gift.

There is a section in *The United Methodist Hymnal* devoted to hymns of invitation. Why invite persons if they are not free to come? We sing these hymns because people have a choice, given in God's grace as free will.

> Take away our bent to sinning; Alpha and Omega be;
> end of faith, as its beginning, set our hearts at liberty.

Another question: Why would someone not choose to accept Christ's gift of salvation?

23. Can a person really become perfect?

In most contexts, this seems like a ridiculous question. Of course, no one can be perfect. Of course not; we are only human.

The problem with that view, John Wesley said, is that Jesus meant it when he said, "Be perfect, therefore, as your heavenly Father is perfect" (Matt. 5:48). Wesley based his sermon "Christian Perfection" on Philippians 3:12, a reminder from Paul to keep moving toward perfection ("I press on to make it my own"). Hebrews 6:1 is an instruction toward perfection. The Collect for Purity, prayed in many denominational traditions, pleads: "Cleanse the thoughts of our hearts by the inspiration of your Holy Spirit, that we may perfectly love you. . . ." The first commandment given by our Lord is to love God with *all* of your heart, soul, and mind (Matt. 22:37). The challenge of Jesus is to perfect love of God and neighbor. That is the meaning of Christian perfection. (Because such a life would be fully holy, sometimes the term "entire sanctification" is used as an alternative name for Christian perfection.)

This teaching continues in United Methodist practice. Every man or woman who is being considered for admission as a full clergy member of an annual conference is asked: "Are you going on to perfection? Do you expect to be made perfect in love in this life?" The appropriate answers are "Yes" and "Yes."

In the twenty-first century, we tend to think of perfection as meaning "without error." Not so for Wesley. He understood that Christian perfection did not mean that one is sinless or free from ignorance or always wise in judgment. Even perfected people need forgiveness! So, what is Christian perfection, this entire sanctification?

For United Methodists, perfection is full love of God and neighbor. Can a Christian expect (look forward to) that gift? John Wesley preached that God intends us to love fully (Matt. 22:37, for example) and God is able to do what God intends. To deny the possibility of perfection is to deny God's power to give the gifts God wants to give.

The Christian life is a journey toward perfection. Even entire sanctification is not an arrival point; instead, it is a mark of growth on a path, as sinful people intend to love God fully and to love neighbor fully. Wesley taught that a few persons come to this maturity in this life (he never claimed it for himself), and he taught that it was also possible for a person to fall from such grace. The Confession of Faith (article XI) points out that the gift of perfection might be received gradually or instantaneously.

At one point, John Wesley declared that proclaiming Christian perfection might well have been the reason God raised up the people called Methodists. Indeed, it is one way to make clear that the gift of saving grace makes a difference in how one lives, going on to perfection.

> A heart in every thought renewed and full of love divine,
> perfect and right and pure and good, a copy, Lord, of thine.

Another question: Are you going on to perfection?

24. What happens when we die?

It was said of early Methodists: "Methodists know how to die well." This means that those believers faced the enemy, death, with calmness and readiness. One tradition says that John Wesley's last words were "The best of all is, God is with us." That is dying well. Philip William Otterbein said on his deathbed: "Jesus. Jesus—I die, but thou livest, and soon I will live with thee." That reflects a sure knowledge that God does not desert God's own when the harbingers of death come to do their work.

Romans 6:23 spells out the contrast between God and death: "For the wages of sin is death, but the free gift of God is eternal life in Christ Jesus our Lord." In his *Explanatory Notes* commentary on Romans 5:12 ("Death came through sin, and so death spread to all because all have sinned."), John Wesley writes that there was no death when there was no sin. Death came because Adam (all of us?) sinned. These are theological statements, not biological statements.

Even though death is an enemy of God (and threatens us with separation from God), the biblical witness is clear that nothing, not even death, is able to separate us from God's love (Rom. 8:38–39). No wonder the United Methodist tradition is one of holy, expectant dying. The promise of John 11:25 ("Those who believe in me, even though they die, will live") is read at almost every funeral among United Methodist people. The official United Methodist service of death and resurrection begins: "Dying, Christ destroyed our death. Rising, Christ restored our life." (See questions 63 and 64 for exploration into heaven and hell as signs of fellowship with God or brokenness from God.)

Death is a confrontation with our own personal mortality because, even though a dying person is surrounded by family and friends and even by the presence of God, we all still die one at a time and in that sense alone. Death is real and complete. The New Testament does not speak of a natural immortality of the soul, as if we never actually die. It speaks of resurrection of the body, the claim that is made each time we state the historic Apostles' Creed and the classic Nicene Creed. (For the words of these creeds, see *UMH* 880–882.)

Paul recognizes the difficulty of "seeing on the other side." In 1 Thessalonians 4:13–14, he pens assurance that the God who raised Jesus from the dead will do the same for the "brothers and sisters." What does such a resurrected body look like? It is a spiritual body (1 Cor. 15:44). In order to be immortal—have eternal life—we must put on immortality (1 Cor. 15:53); it is a new gift from God. The one who has created us will create us again! (2 Cor. 5:17). There is much we do not grasp by our limited vision (for example, Matt. 22:30), but we know that whatever it is, it is what God knows to be best. Such life begins now.

> Ten thousand to their endless home this solemn moment fly,
> and we are to the margin come, and we expect to die.
> E'en now by faith we join our hands with those that went before,
> And greet the blood-besprinkled bands on the eternal shore.

Another question: What is the difference between immortality of the soul and resurrection of the body?

5

Salvation

 25. What is prevenient, justifying, and sanctifying grace?

John Wesley said salvation was like a house. "Our main doctrines, which include all the rest, are three: that of repentance, of faith, and of holiness. The first of these we account, as it were, the porch of religion; the next, the door; the third is religion itself" (*Works,* vol. 9, p. 227).

The first part of the journey to salvation is repentance (Matt. 4:17). (Wesley calls this the porch of the house.) Repentance is more than regret for sin; it involves turning in a new direction. We can become aware of our need to repent only when God's grace stirs that awareness within us. God's grace makes the first move. In the Wesleyan heritage, that initial gift of grace is called "prevenient grace." ("Prevenient" means "going before.") This teaching emphasizes a connection between the moral law and our salvation; but because prevenient grace from God moves us to repent, this repentance is not our good works, but God's gracious activity in us.

The next part of the journey toward salvation is faith (Rom. 5:1). (Wesley calls this the door of the house.) It is this faith in Jesus Christ that justifies us (Gal. 3:24). Think of justifying the margins of a text you are typing on your computer. You line up the margins. Justification is getting lined up right with God. It is not something we do on our own; faith itself is a gift, and since it justifies us with God, the gift is called "justifying grace." Is this done quickly or gradually? The answer is "Yes" and "Yes." Philip William Otterbein was asked how he came to be brought to the gospel; he replied, "By degrees was I brought to the knowledge of the truth." Note the phrase "was . . . brought." Justification is not something we do; it is something God does for us.

The third part of John Wesley's image of the house is holy living; the house itself is holy living. Getting justified does not complete the journey. Once we pass through the door (by grace), we are in the house where our lives are to be lived in accord with God's command that we love one another (1 John 3:11). We are not able to do such good works on our own; God's grace makes it possible for us to be sanctified (live holy lives). This gift is called "sanctifying" grace. United Methodists sometimes are accused of emphasizing good works at the expense of faith. Not so! There is nothing in our teachings to argue that we are saved by works. What is clear in United Methodist thought is that where there is faith there are good works (James 2:17). Repentance (porch). Justification (door). Sanctification, holy living (the house itself)—all possible by God's grace.

> Let us plead for faith alone, faith which by our works is shown;
> God it is who justifies, only faith the grace applies.

Another question: Which part of Wesley's "house of salvation" is most difficult for you?

 26. What about repentance?

"When did you repent?" In the United Methodist tradition, a believer might well answer that question, "This morning, yesterday, the day before, the day before that, ten years ago, and five years before that." Repentance is an ongoing part of sanctification, seeking to live a holy life. Persons in the Wesleyan and Otterbein traditions are not likely to recognize a "one time fits all" kind of repentance.

True repentance (which is more than regret at "getting caught") expresses itself in holy living. John the Baptist challenged those who came to him for the baptism of repentance: "Bear fruit worthy of repentance" (Matt. 3:8). This emphasis in Wesley on repentance and works does not dilute the statement in the Articles of Religion (article IX) that justification is "by faith, and not for our own works or deservings. . . . We are justified by faith, only." United Methodists seek to live out the fruit of that faith: ". . . good works, which are the fruits of faith, and follow after justification . . . spring out of a true and lively faith, insomuch that by them a lively faith may be as evidently known as a tree is discovered by its fruit" (article X of the Articles of Religion). (Look at Rev. 2:5.)

Repentance and the good works that follow repentance are not the cause of salvation. Wesley (in remarking on Matt. 3:8) described two kinds of repentance: (a) legal—which is conviction of sin, and (b) evangelical—which is a change of heart from all sin to all holiness. In this framework, the life of good works is never very far from the life of faith.

Prevenient grace (see question 25) is God's presence even before one comes to faith. Such grace is in every life and circumstance, even among those we would label nonbelievers. The truth is that God's love simply gets there first. This is God's work, and to be done in God's good time. For that reason, Wesley (from the Methodist side of the family) and Martin Boehm and Jacob Albright and Philip William Otterbein (from the Evangelical United Brethren branch) did not usually proffer long, extended, emotional appeals to "come to Jesus." (In later times, some leaders in the tradition did adopt this sense of pleading.) For the early leaders of what is now United Methodism, God was the actor in salvation; God was the mover toward repentance; God was the initiator of grace, so human manipulation had no place. We repent because God has gotten to us (Rom. 2:4; Acts 11:18; 2 Pet. 3:9)!

> Now incline me to repent, let me now my sins lament,
> now my foul revolt deplore, weep, believe, and sin no more.

Another question: Why is it easier for most persons to repent in private rather than in public?

27. Can a person backslide?

Once we are captured by God's grace, can we fall away? Is God's hold on us so secure that we are "once saved, always saved"? In some religious communities (Presbyterian and some Baptists, for example) there is a belief in the doctrine of "perseverance of the saints," sometimes called "eternal security." This teaching holds that the Holy Spirit does not allow true believers to slip from God's grasp.

United Methodists do not hold that view. There is too much evidence of the possibility of backsliding! King Saul seemed to run hot and cold (1 Sam. 10:9–24). Demas abandoned Paul because Demas fell in love with the world (2 Tim. 4:10). The message to the church at Ephesus was that it had fallen away from the love it first had for the Lord (Rev. 2:4). One of our Lord's close disciples betrayed him (Matt. 26:14–16). King David moves from sacred leadership to participate in adultery and murder (2 Sam. 11). Jesus acknowledged that Peter's faith would fail (Luke 22:31–34, 54–62). John Mark deserted the ministry he shared with Paul (Acts 15:37–38). Paul wrote the Corinthian church to stop quarreling and to get its act together (1 Cor. 1:11–17).

The evidence of backsliding is not limited to the Bible! (One can recall that Joseph Stalin trained for the priesthood and that Adolph Hitler professed Christian faith.) As long as God chooses to give us freedom (see question 22), we have the choice of walking away. Article XII ("Of Sin after Justification") of the Articles of Religion is forthright: "After we have received the Holy Ghost, we may depart from grace given, and fall into sin, and by the grace of God rise again and amend our lives." The Confession of Faith is equally strong: "We believe, although we have experienced regeneration, it is possible to depart from grace and fall into sin, and we may even then, by the grace of God, be renewed in righteousness."

The United Methodist legacy is that faith expresses itself in faithful works. The absence of these expressions of love of neighbor sends a signal that faith itself might be absent. If there is no faith, there is no salvation. But, praise the Lord, the opportunity to repent and be restored to faith is as present as the offering of God's grace.

Because of this teaching, United Methodists often speak of the way of salvation (*via salutis*) instead of the order of salvation (*ordo salutis*). Instead of a straight line and order, "the way of salvation" suggests a journey with starts and stops, reversals and repentance. And God is with us all the way.

> I my Master have denied, I afresh have crucified,
> oft profaned his hallowed name, put him to an open shame.

Another question: Why does God allow Christians to backslide?

28. What does it mean to be born again?

We are, of course, not the first to ask this question. Nicodemus came to Jesus with the same inquiry: "How can anyone be born after having grown old?" (John 3:4) Jesus told him that one must be born from above. (The Greek word can mean either "born again" or "born from above.") The term used in United Methodist theology is "new birth." What is this new birth?

When a believer dies to sin, he or she is born to new life in Christ. The new birth is the journey toward sanctification (holy living). It starts with God's gift of grace at justification. (To go back to the house image in question 25, it is a move through the door into the house.) This is sometimes called regeneration, because it is a new start.

The Articles of Religion instruct us that baptism is a sign of this new birth. That new birth can be given in the sacrament of baptism, certainly in the case of infants who are baptized. (See question 40.) In the case of persons of "riper years," the gift of the new birth (being born again) is simultaneous with the gift of faith, of justification. For adults, Wesley was clear that baptism and the new birth were not the same. "[New birth] is that great change which God works in the soul when he brings it into life, when he raises it from the death of sin to the life of righteousness" (*Works,* vol. 2, pp. 193–94). For adults, the new birth begins with belief.

The new birth is necessary for salvation because it marks the move toward holiness. That comes with faith. Holiness is the essence of the journey. ("Pursue peace with everyone, and the holiness without which no one will see the Lord" [Heb. 12:14].) With the gift of new birth ("born from above"), we move to align our lives with God's will. This is God's change of "sinner" into "saint."

Of course, even a baby that is born must grow up. United Methodists celebrate the new birth in infants and in adults, but in both cases there is rejoicing when those persons live in the light where "it may be clearly seen that their deeds have been done in God" (John 3:21). Jesus said all of this birth and growth is a mystery of the Spirit's gift of new life. "The wind blows where it chooses, and you hear the sound of it, but you do not know where it comes from or where it goes. So it is with everyone who is born of the Spirit" (John 3:8). In light of that word from our Lord, we do well to be cautious about identifying any one way as the way God gives this gift!

> Almighty God of truth and love, to me thy power impart;
> the mountain from my soul remove, the hardness from my heart.
> O may the least omission pain my reawakened soul,
> and drive me to that blood again, which makes the wounded whole.

Another question: What difference does the new birth make in a life?

29. What do good works have to do with salvation?

Everything and nothing.

"We believe good works are the necessary fruits of faith and follow regeneration but they do not have the virtue to remove our sins or to avert divine judgment" (article X, Confession of Faith). United Methodists are in the train of the Protestant Reformation in declaring that salvation is by faith alone. One distinctive clarification of that truth, however, is the Wesleyan assertion that salvation means transformation, and transformation means moral behavior. Works are how "faith is made evident" (Confession of Faith). To put it bluntly: good works won't save you, but if you are saved there will be good works.

Philip William Otterbein and Martin Boehm were the initial superintendents of the United Brethren (who later became part of the Evangelical United Brethren Church and whose values eventually helped form The United Methodist Church). They presided at an 1802 meeting of the Conference of the United Brethren when one action was the approval of John Miller to "exhort the people to incite them to good works as much as he can through God's grace." Themes common to all the streams of United Methodism can be found here: grace and good works. By the gifts of God, God's people are not only forgiven, but are called to action (James 2:14–17).

In John Wesley's sermon "Scriptural Christianity," he points to the example of Jesus (John 5:17) who said, "I also am working."

Wesley calls the roll of the judgment Jesus makes on those who do not work to feed the hungry, clothe the naked, help the orphaned, support the stranger, visit those who are in prison, and assist the sick (Matt. 25:31–46). Doing good works is a serious matter, because those who fail to do these things are slated for eternal punishment (Matt. 25:46).

Some of the energy in the way that Otterbein and Wesley vigorously insisted on including holy living (sanctification, good works) in their accounting of salvation came from a theological debate between them and Calvinists. (See question 30.) The leaders of the Methodist movement and its companion communities (Evangelical and United Brethren) feared that persons who believed in predestination might go to an extreme and figure that their moral lives made no difference because they were already saved by God's choice. Even though that was a caricature of the Calvinist theology, the roots began to grow for the United Methodist practice of including righteous living in the fullness of salvation.

> Active faith that lives within, conquers hell and death and sin,
> hallows whom it first made whole, forms the Savior in the soul.

Another question: What would you say to someone who says, "I don't need to believe; I live a good life"?

 30. Who can be saved?

United Methodists believe that all persons have access to the saving grace of Jesus Christ. (This view is known as "universal atonement," as opposed to "limited atonement.") The passion of John 3:16 ("that everyone who believes in him may not perish but may have eternal life") forms a foundation for this teaching.

The offer of salvation is to be extended to all humankind (Acts 2:38). The light of Christ is intended for all (John 1:9). The power of God for salvation is to everyone who has faith (Rom. 1:16). Much of the vigor of John Wesley's insistence on the universal availability of salvation came from his reaction against extreme forms of predestination, a teaching shaped by Augustine (fourth and fifth centuries) and John Calvin (sixteenth century). Although a moderate interpretation of predestination held that God elected (predestined) for salvation anyone who would believe, Wesley made impassioned attack against the idea of double predestination (if God elects some for salvation, God must elect others for damnation). Double predestination flew in the face of free will (see question 22) and in the face of the universality of Christ's love.

In 1785, Philip William Otterbein led his Reformed congregation in Baltimore (predecessor to the United Brethren) to declare that no preacher could stay among them who taught predestination or who taught the doctrine of eternal security (see question 27). Students of John Wesley have noted at least five cases he made against predestination: (1) If God has predetermined who is saved, all preaching is vain. (2) Predestination does away with the need for Christian revelation and practice, because nothing could change the eternal decree of God. (3) Predestination destroys any enthusiasm for good works. (4) Predestination is based on a very few biblical passages, and those passages are against the "the whole scope and tenor of Scripture." (5) Predestination makes God into a false, unjust one who condemns many who earnestly desire salvation. (This summary is based on Lovett Weems, *John Wesley's Message Today*, p. 29.)

In John Wesley's sermon "Awake, Thou That Sleepest," the preacher pointed to 1 Timothy 1:15 ("Christ Jesus came into the world to save sinners") and to Philippians 2:12 ("Work out your own salvation with fear and trembling"). In his *Explanatory Notes,* Wesley underlines the teaching of universal grace, the offer of salvation to everyone: "Save sinners: all sinners, without exception." With prevenient grace (see question 25), God is already at work to apply that salvation. United Methodists still proclaim that good news and invitation to all.

Come, sinners, to the gospel feast; let every soul be Jesus' guest.
Ye need not one be left behind, for God hath bid all humankind.

Another question: What is the relationship between "universal grace" and evangelism?

6

Church

31. What is the nature of the church?

My wife, Toni, and I attend Bethany United Methodist Church on Guess Road in Durham, North Carolina. Is that the church?

We take part in the Lizzie Grey Chandler Sunday school class. Is that the church?

I am a clergy member in full connection with the North Carolina Conference of The United Methodist Church. Is that the church?

I am a member of the House of Delegates of the North Carolina Council of Churches. Is that the church?

I am part of a denomination that is a member of both the National Council of Churches and the World Council of Churches. Is that the church?

Not so long ago, I preached at First Presbyterian Church. Before that, I preached at St. Philip's Episcopal Church and at First Baptist Church. Is that the church?

United Methodists understand that the church is both visible and invisible. Visibly, the church has three presenting qualities: preaching of the pure Word of God, due administration of the sacraments, and the presence of people of faith (article XIII of the Articles of Religion). Without faith, there is no church. Without preaching, faith would fade away. Without the sacraments, we would be without God's means of grace.

There are four dimensions (or notes) to the church: one, holy, catholic, and apostolic (article V, Confession of Faith).

The church is one (John 17:21). The unity of the church is in Jesus Christ.

The church is holy (1 Pet. 2:5). The church is called to be a set-apart, different kind of people.

The church is catholic (Eph. 2:14). The church is a universal community beyond human boundaries. (The word "catholic" means universal and does not refer to just one branch of the church.)

The church is apostolic (Acts 2:42). The church teaches what the apostles taught and is in solidarity with the apostolic witness.

United Methodists understand that the church is also a community of discipline. ("Discipline" has the same root as "disciple.") The framework in which United Methodists live out their Christian discipleship is called *The Book of Discipline* (see question 73). The General Rules (by which one exhibits a desire for salvation) are protected from change by the Constitution of The United Methodist Church; these General Rules make clear both expectation and accountability in the disciplined life of the church. (The General Rules begin on *BOD*, p. 71.)

The church is the body of Christ (Eph. 4:1–16), in which there are many gifts for ministry (1 Cor. 12:4). The church is a varied community (1 Cor. 12:12–31). The church is one body throughout the world (Eph. 4:4). The church is the communion of saints, both living and dead (1 John 1:3; Eph. 2:19–20).

The church erupts into the world wherever the body of Christ erupts into the world. Baptism is the common mark on those who enter into this household of faith (Gal. 3:27). John Wesley recognized how varied the church might look, so in his sermon "Catholic Spirit" he was expansive in his description of church: "friends, as [kindred] in the Lord, as members of Christ and children of God, as joint partakers now of the present kingdom of God, and fellow-heirs of [God's] eternal kingdom, all . . . who believe in the Lord Jesus Christ, who love God and [humankind]" (*Works*, vol. 2, p. 94).

> Many are we now, and one, we who Jesus have put on;
> there is neither bond nor free, male nor female, Lord, in thee.

Another question: How do you experience church?

32. What is the mission of the church?

The *Book of Discipline of The United Methodist Church 2004* has a direct answer to this question: "The mission of the church is to make disciples of Jesus Christ . . . by proclaiming the good news of God's grace and by exemplifying Jesus' command to love God and neighbor, thus seeking the fulfillment of God's reign and realm in the world" (from *BOD*, ¶s 120, 121). In carrying out this mission, the church does a better job at some times than at other times, but there is always the confidence that nothing can destroy the church (Matt. 16:18).

The United Methodist Church declares that although the annual conference is the basic body of the church (see question 74), the local church is the most "significant arena" for the task of disciple making. (Some United Methodists think this emphasis on the local church is an erosion of the connectional witness of the church; see question 36.) In a sense, local churches are to measure themselves against mission. What does that look like?

The church's mission is the transformation of the world. Such transformation occurs when there is faithful proclamation (Rom. 10:14). Such transformation occurs when there is gracious hospitality (Heb. 13:2). Such transformation occurs when persons are led into faith commitment and baptized (Acts 2:38). Such transformation occurs when there is nurture through spiritual disciplines and holy conferencing (Acts 2:42). Such transformation occurs when persons are sent into the world to serve (James 2:14–17; Matt. 25:31–46). Such transformation occurs when the church is intentional in seeking to gather persons into the community of Christ (Matt. 28:19–20).

In one place (*BOD*, ¶131), United Methodists are called to live in mission with "active expectancy." Here is blended the balance that is so often characteristic of United Methodism: (a) "active"—our human efforts—and (b) "expectancy"—awareness that it is God who acts. The mission of the church is finally God's mission.

> Let us for each other care, each the other's burdens bear;
> to thy church the pattern give, show how true believers live.

Another question: What is the church's mission when "the world" does not want to hear the gospel?

33. What are the creeds of the church?

A creed is a statement of belief (the Latin word *credo* means "I believe"). Such declarations have emerged in the church's life from time to time, most often as an effort to head off false teachings. The United Methodist Church views Scripture as the supreme authority in matters of faith and morals. Even so, the historic creeds have been, for many United Methodists, clear affirmation of biblical truth.

John Wesley edited the Articles of Religion of the Church of England before he sent them as a standard for American Methodism. One of the portions Wesley omitted was the article sanctioning three creeds as definitive documents for the church: the Apostles' Creed, the Nicene Creed, and the Athanasian Creed. Thus, even though early Methodists accepted the theology of the creeds, they did not make them formal assertions of the faith. (Toward the end of the twentieth century, United Methodists did agree to the Nicene Creed in accepting the *Church of Christ Uniting Consensus*, a major ecumenical project.)

In practice, United Methodists draw on several creedal declarations. *The United Methodist Hymnal* includes the Nicene Creed, two versions of the Apostles' Creed, a statement of faith of the United Church of Canada, a statement of faith of the Korean Methodist Church, a Modern Affirmation, the World Methodist Social Affirmation, and three affirmations based on New Testament passages. It is significant to note that only the two historic credos (Nicene and Apostles') carry the title "creed."

The Apostles' Creed, originally used for inquiry of candidates for baptism, is in the United Methodist liturgy for the baptismal covenant. The Nicene Creed, developed as a theological response to those in the fourth century who questioned the divine and human nature of Jesus, appears in the language of both the Articles of Religion and the Confession of Faith. Clearly, even though the demand for affirming these creeds is not in United Methodist standards of doctrine (see question 49), United Methodists accept and celebrate the teachings of these ancient pronouncements.

I have a friend who closes his mouth when he does not agree with part of one of the creeds being used in worship. (He has particular trouble with the virgin birth—see question 8.) I encourage him to join with the congregation in full recitation of the creed, first as an act of humility that the whole church knows more than any individual, and second as an act of expectancy, anticipating his continued growth into the fullness of the gospel. (He is not impressed with my advice, and asks me where would we Protestants be if Martin Luther had accepted what most of the church believed? In fact, the Reformation was needed because the church was failing to live by the doctrines spelled out in the creeds.)

Creed statements can be bound by the limits of language and the specifics of a given time, but they become appropriate tests of how the church has (or has not) drifted from the apostolic faith.

> E'en now we think and speak the same, and cordially agree,
> concentered all, through Jesus' name, in perfect harmony.

Another question: Why do some congregations regularly omit use of the creeds?

34. Who are clergy?

In my part of the country, clergy are often referred to as "preacher." In other parts of the nation, clergy are called "pastor." Or "Reverend" or "minister" or "Hey, you!" or, on a bad day, "that incompetent slob who is ruining everything we have tried to do." Hmmm.

In The United Methodist Church, clergy are those persons who are ordained, commissioned, or licensed for a set-apart, representative servant leadership role. The annual conference—not the local church—is the authorizing and electing body for each of these relationships. There are educational, spiritual, experiential, character, and gift requirements for each status. Clergy remain accountable to the annual conference.

There are two categories of ordained clergy: elders and deacons. Elders are set apart for preaching the Word, ordering the church for mission (external life) and ministry (internal life), administering the sacraments, and ministries of service (Titus 1:5–9; 1 Cor. 11:23). Deacons are set apart for the proclamation of the Word and service that connects congregational life with community life (Acts 6:1–6; 1 Tim. 3:8–13).

In some traditions, there are three orders of ordained clergy: priests (elders), deacons, and bishops. John Wesley led Methodist people to understand that the New Testament bishop is the same order as priest (elder). Consequently, United Methodists give a special function to bishops, but do not ordain them to a separate order. They remain elders.

Commissioned ministers are those who are in process of moving toward ordination and full conference membership (see question 74). Licensed pastors are unordained persons who are authorized to serve the full pastoral role (including the sacraments) in the particular place to which they are appointed (and nowhere else). The development of the office of licensed local pastor (unordained) is an example of the practical nature of United Methodist life: What do we have to do to get the job done?

Conference membership is another aspect of clergy life. United Methodist clergy are not members of local churches; they are members of the annual conference. (They might be full members, probationary members, or associate members.) Only elders and deacons in full connection have full right of voice and vote on all matters (except for electing laypersons to jurisdictional and General conferences—see question 74.) After consultation with all parties concerned, the bishop appoints the clergy to their places of service. Both men and women are eligible for any clergy relationship in United Methodism.

John Wesley did not argue that the Methodist way of organizing the life of the church was the only biblical way, but he did insist that the polity of the Methodist people was an obvious New Testament way of "doing church." As changes and new models of design occur, United Methodists seek to remain biblical in thrust and pattern.

My talents, gifts, and graces, Lord, into thy blessed hands receive;
and let me live to preach thy word, and let me to thy glory live;
my every sacred moment spend in publishing the sinner's Friend.

Another question: What would the church be like without clergy?

35. What is the role of laypersons?

"*All* Christians are called through their baptism to this ministry of servanthood in the world to the glory of God and for human fulfillment" (*BOD*, ¶125). That clarion invitation to ministry does not leave much hiding place for laypersons! "That's the pastor's job!" or "I have done enough already!" or "Who, me?" do not hold up too well against baptismal challenge.

Jacob Albright, the beginning influence for the Evangelical Association—in the Evangelical United Brethren stream of United Methodism—was a layperson in the early days of the movement. Martin Boehm, who later joined with Philip William Otterbein to form the United Brethren, was a Mennonite farmer well into adulthood. In order to have preachers for the rapidly developing Methodist preaching houses, John Wesley sent out lay preachers as early as the 1740s. Francis Asbury spent years guiding Methodism in the United States as a layman before being ordained in 1784. Today's United Methodism guarantees an equal number of lay members and clergy members of the annual conference (and the jurisdictional conference and the General Conference). The conference lay leader may sit with the bishop's cabinet (and in at least the North Carolina annual conference, sits with the bishop at the president's table). A layperson always chairs the church council of a local United Methodist congregation and, although not absolutely required, almost inevitably laity form the total membership of the trustees. Men and women are chosen for all of these positions.

The reason for this strong and continuing role for laypersons is clear: we are in this together. The Protestant Reformation's term for this relationship is "priesthood of all believers." This phrase operates at two levels: (a) each person stands before God without intermediary—priesthood of each believer, and (b) all of us in our life together form a commonly held priesthood—priesthood of all believers. In this regard, the Scripture makes no distinction between lay and clergy (Exod. 19:5–6; 1 Pet. 2:9; Rev. 5:10).

The gifts vary (1 Cor. 12:4–11). The response to the call varies (Rev. 3:14–22). Yet, the demands of the gospel are the same (1 Pet. 4:7–11). Yet, the mission of the Master is the same (Luke 10:1–2).

In spelling out the General Rules (for how the early Methodist societies would function), John Wesley acknowledged the multiple ways in which the lives of laity impact (or do not) the world with the gospel; the General Rules name issues such as working on the Sabbath, drunkenness, slaveholding, avoiding taxes, wearing costly clothes, borrowing with no expectation of paying back—circumstances from the daily lives of the laypeople who formed those Methodist societies. Lay ministry was much more than "doing things around the church." Lay ministry involved gospel collision with the world!

The task thy wisdom hath assigned, O let me cheerfully fulfill;
in all my works thy presence find, and prove thy good and perfect will.

Another question: What would the church be like without laity?

 ## 36. What is connectionalism?

The spell-checker on my computer says there is no such word as "connectionalism." United Methodists would not agree.

John Wesley called the budding Methodist movement in England "the connexion." All the terms used to talk about Methodist life were words like conference, band, society, classes, covenant, council. What do they have in common? They are all relational words, connectional words, if you will. "Connecting" is how United Methodists live out the gospel.

The Book of Discipline (¶130) speaks of "the journey of a connectional people," and describes that tradition as "multi-leveled, global in scope, and local in thrust." In other words, it happens everywhere United Methodism happens. One way that expresses itself is in church membership: when one affiliates with a local United Methodist congregation, one not only joins that one church, but joins the entire denomination.

What do we do together? There is a common faith tradition. We share a single Constitution. There is the leadership of a Council of Bishops. There is a mutually determined, common mission. Finances and other resources are pooled in order to do more together than any single entity could do alone. We share our clergy within the connection. We submit ourselves to "what is best for us" rather than "what is best for me." (The question at the heart of the matter is: What is best for sharing the gospel?) The sense is that each of us can better see the whole picture if we each tell the other what we are seeing. That's why we confer—hold conference (see question 74). The word *episkopos*—bishop, superintendent—means "one who has oversight, can see the whole picture." The episcopal form of government—with bishops—is an expression of a connectional understanding of church; we need to see the whole picture, not just what can be seen from our particular spots on the map.

The New Testament church was well aware of the connectional way of being disciples. The Jerusalem conference (Acts 15:1–21) was a connectional conversation about circumcision. The sending of the apostles and elders to tell of the decision about circumcision (Acts 15:22–31) was a connectional use of personnel resources. The example of the churches in Macedonia going together to help the poor (2 Cor. 8:1–7) was a connectional model for sharing finances. The description in 1 Timothy of the qualifications of bishops (elders) and deacons (1 Tim. 3:1–13) was a connectional statement of accountability.

In United Methodism, there are structures that tie local congregations to districts and districts to regional annual conferences and annual conferences to jurisdictional/central conferences and all of these to a General Conference. (See question 74.) It is a "vital web of interactive relationships." It is connectionalism.

> He bids us build each other up; and, gathered into one,
> to our high calling's glorious hope we hand in hand go on.

Another question: What are the dangers in a connectional system?

7

Worship and Sacraments

 37. How do United Methodists worship?

Come with me on a quick tour of six United Methodist congregations. Within just a few miles of each other, they are places where my wife and I worshiped when I first retired.

Church A: A lively praise band gave volume and vigor to a service in which most of us were clapping, singing, and swaying. God was present.

Church B: The traditional hymns shared time with more contemporary songs, and the pastor read an insightful sermon. God was present.

Church C: The call-and-response shouts of encouragement to the preacher and the choir (which sang a rap anthem) captured a spirit of excitement. God was present.

Church D: As is this congregation's weekly practice, members of all ages came to partake of the Lord's Supper. God was present.

Church E: Informality ("Let's sing Happy Birthday to Jim") and routine guided a warm and unsurprising service. God was present.

Church F: After a long procession, the choir sang an introit in Latin, and the congregation followed the order carefully in the hymnal. God was present.

United Methodists have a basic pattern for worship (*UMH*, pp. 2–5, for example) but United Methodists must have taken very seriously the injunction in the Articles of Religion that "it is not necessary that rites and ceremonies should in all places be the same," and have listened to the counsel of the Confession of Faith that "[public worship] may be modified by the church according to circumstances and the needs of [the people]."

On the other hand, few United Methodists have heard the equally passionate advice of the Articles of Religion: "Whosoever, through his private judgment, willingly and purposely doth openly break the rites and ceremonies of the church to which he belongs . . . ought to be rebuked openly." Hmmm.

Important questions to be asked about worship are: (1) Who is the God being worshiped? and (2) Who are the people being formed? Those two questions make some of the tension for those who shape decisions about United Methodist worship. On the one hand is the teaching of nineteenth-century Danish philosopher Søren Kirkegaard: worship is aimed at God and is solely for the glory of God. On the other hand, second-century church leader Irenaeus noted, "The glory of God is humanity fully alive," so the way of bringing glory to God has been the transformation of humans into beings pleasing to God.

The Bible says, "O come, let us worship and bow down, let us kneel before the LORD, our Maker!" (Ps. 95:6). But the Bible also says: "Is not this the fast that I choose: to loose the bonds of injustice, to undo the thongs of the yoke, to let the oppressed go free, and to break every yoke?" (Isa. 58:6).

United Methodists have tried to maintain this balance in a number of ways, sometimes emphasizing one, sometimes emphasizing the other. There is a *Book of Worship*, but it is designed more for those who plan worship than it is for weekly use in the pew. There is a *United Methodist Hymnal*, but congregations feel free to add to its material by turning to other sources for music.

There is no one way that United Methodists worship, but the questions always remain: When we worship as we do, who is the God we worship? When we worship as we do, who are the kind of people being formed?

O for a thousand tongues to sing my great Redeemer's praise,
    the glories of my God and King, the triumphs of his grace!

Another question: How do you define "worship"?

38. Is it a table or an altar?

Although many United Methodists use the words "altar" and "table" interchangeably, there are some theological reasons to choose the word "table." An altar is a place where sacrifices are made; United Methodists believe that Christ's sacrifice on the cross is the only sacrifice needed for our salvation. ("The offering of Christ, once made, is that perfect redemption, propitiation, and satisfaction for all the sins of the whole world," article XX, Articles of Religion.) If there is no need for further sacrifice, what use do we have of an altar?

During the nineteenth-century revivals and camp meetings, Methodists and United Brethren and Evangelicals called people to sacrifice their own lives to God (Rom. 12:1). This invitation became known as the altar call, and the place where people came to make those commitments was then called "the altar." It was not much of a stretch for people to begin to refer to the Lord's Table as an altar.

The language of the *United Methodist Book of Worship* and *The United Methodist Hymnal* is "Lord's Table." In John Wesley's sermon on "The Duty of Constant Communion," Wesley refers to the "holy table" (*Works,* vol. 3, p. 429). Philip William Otterbein, in his guidelines for the German Reformed Church in Baltimore, uses the term "Lord's Table." This usage magnifies the fact that this is a family meal with our Lord as host.

If our Lord is host, he must be present! The theological language for this reality is "real presence." Unlike Roman Catholic tradition, which speaks of transubstantiation—the bread and wine are changed in substance to the body and blood of Jesus; and unlike the Lutheran teaching of consubstantiation, which instructs that Jesus is in, with, and under the bread and wine; and unlike the Anabaptist understanding that this meal is simply a memorial of something that happened "back then," with Christ only symbolically present now, the United Methodist claim and experience is that our Lord is really present as a spiritual presence. It is no less real because it is spiritual, because United Methodists believe spiritual reality is real!

The instruction "Do this in remembrance of me" (1 Cor. 11:24) is a call to form the body of Jesus again (to re-member is to put the members together again). In so doing, we claim his presence with us even now. That presence points to a coming banquet (Matt. 8:11; Mark 14:25; Luke 22:18) where the whole family of God will gather in joy. No wonder that Holy Communion is the most frequent act of Christians at worship around the world!

O the depth of love divine, the unfathomable grace!
Who shall say how bread and wine God into us conveys!
How the bread his flesh imparts, how the wine transmits his blood,
fills his faithful people's hearts with all the life of God!

Another question: What memory, if any, do you have of the first time you took Communion?

 ### 39. How often do United Methodists take Communion (and other questions)?

The General Conference of The United Methodist Church has encouraged local churches to study a return to a practice of weekly Communion at the main service of worship. Part of the eighteenth-century Wesleyan revival in England was a push to get the Church of England to draw again from New Testament roots and to resume frequent Communion. (The Anglican Church in that day was spasmodic in offering the Lord's Table.) Wesley thought the New Testament called for "constant Communion." It is the plain command of Christ (Luke 22:19). It is a means of receiving the grace of God and being pardoned for our sins, a new covenant made possible by the gift of the cross (1 Cor. 11:25–26). Wesley said the early Christians communed almost daily, and certainly always at the Lord's Day service.

Wesley hoped that Methodists in America would have the Lord's Supper regularly, but there were no ordained clergy to serve. Once there were a few elders ordained, they could only come around quarterly, in their superintending roles. The Methodists called them "presiding elders," not because they presided at the business table, but because they presided at the Lord's Table. (That title, presiding elder, stayed with the church until more recent times named that office "district superintendent.") The habit of quarterly Communion began to work its way into Methodist life.

Many United Methodist congregations have Communion monthly, and a few have begun to move toward weekly celebration. Some have maintained the quarterly tradition that was once necessitated by absence of clergy.

United Methodists describe the elements as bread and wine, but for more than one hundred twenty-five years have chosen to use grape juice instead of wine. This choice reflects a commitment to abstain from alcoholic beverages and brings a social witness to the Table. The use of grape juice opens the Table to children, youth, and those who struggle with the use of alcohol. (As a side note, the Welch grape products were begun by a Methodist layman who discovered a process for preserving unfermented grape juice for his congregation's services.) The use of grape juice is sometimes a problem in ecumenical settings.

Who comes to the Table? The practice has varied over the years. Wesley and Otterbein might close the Table to those not in good spiritual standing. This observance continued in early Methodist and United Brethren days in America. More recently, United Methodists have practiced an open Table, inviting anyone who responded to the invitation (who love Christ, repent of sin, and seek peace). Wesley spoke of the sacrament as a "converting ordinance." Now some United Methodists have called the church to remember that the Lord's Supper is a family meal for those who have been baptized (baptism being initiation into the family). It is not for casual discipleship. For pastoral and evangelical reasons, United Methodists in the United States seldom turn away anyone who comes to the Table. We seek to be good stewards of what is, after all, the Lord's Table.

> Sure and real is the grace, the manner be unknown;
> only meet us in thy ways, and perfect us in one.
> Let us taste the heavenly powers, Lord, we ask for nothing more.
> Thine to bless, 'tis only ours to wonder and adore.

Another question: Why is Communion the most common act of Christians around the world?

40. What about infant baptism?

The Articles of Religion of The Methodist Church and the Confession of Faith of the Evangelical United Brethren Church (the families that make up The United Methodist Church) both affirm the baptism of infants. Why?

The Articles simply state that the practice is to be continued. The Confession says it is because children are under the atonement of Christ and are heirs of the kingdom of God. Such children are to be led to make their own professions of faith in Christ.

In cultures where believer's baptism is the more common practice, United Methodists sometimes refer to infant baptism as "christening." This is inaccurate language. "Christening" is that part of a service in which a name is given. Usage of the term goes back to a time when church records were the official legal records and the recording of the name was an important legal responsibility. Baptism and christening were synonymous. That is no longer the case.

The baptism of an infant is a baptism. (See question 41.) Biblical practice seems to have included both believer's baptism (Acts 2:38; 8:13; 9:18; 22:16) and the baptism of households, including children (Acts 16:15; 16:33; Matt. 19:13–15). Wesley argued that households must have had children and that Jewish Christians would have remembered the Jewish custom of circumcising babies. Children who are baptized before the age of accountability (whatever that is!) are to be nurtured by the covenant community until they come to their own profession of faith.

United Methodists typically baptize (regardless of age) by sprinkling (think of the descent of the Holy Spirit at Pentecost—Luke 3:21–22; Acts 2:38; Acts 19:1–7). There are times when United Methodists baptize by immersion (remember Rom. 6:3–5 and Col. 2:12, as a mark of the death of our old life and resurrection into new life, washing away of sins). Although it is rare, United Methodist practice also allows for baptism by pouring—a large amount of water poured over the head of the candidate (bringing to mind the flowing grace of God [Matt. 3:16; Mark 1:9–10]).

Regardless of the age of the candidate, baptism is initiation into the household of faith, "incorporated by the Holy Spirit into God's new creation." The prime actor is God. Baptism is about what God is doing, rather than about how we are responding. Most Baptist traditions see baptism as a human response to God's love (something you do when you know what you are doing). United Methodists, on the other hand, see baptism as a sign of God's act, a "gift, offered to us without price."

> Thee, Father, Son, and Holy Ghost, let all our hearts receive,
> present with thy celestial host the peaceful answer give;
> to each covenant the blood apply which takes our sins away,
> and register our names on high and keep us to that day!

Another question: What is the role of water in baptism?

41. Can I be rebaptized?

Carlene Paschal rushed up to her pastor. "Praise God!" she began. "I have met God in a new way and I want to recommit my life to Christ. I want to be baptized again as a sign of my new beginning."

Ernesto Perez asked his pastor for "a moment of your time." He began slowly, "You know, Reverend, I've been thinking. I was baptized when I was just a few weeks old. I don't remember anything about it. Now that I am an adult, I'd like to be baptized again—you know, something I can remember."

Harrison Dodge stood on the banks of the Jordan River. He said, "This trip to the Holy Land would be so meaningful if I could be rebaptized, right here in these waters where Jesus was baptized."

What's a United Methodist pastor to do? For starters, he or she will look at *BOD*, ¶341. In that place, there are only seven items listed as "unauthorized conduct" by pastors; one of them is "No pastor shall rebaptize."

The central reason that United Methodists do not practice rebaptism is because of the belief that baptism is about God's action, not our action. Even if we slip and fall from the grace of baptism, God has kept God's promise. Baptism is an instrument of God's initiating love and God does not take that away. It is as if baptism has stamped us with a mark declaring us "property of

God." Even if later years and later experiences hide that mark, it is still there. God writes with indelible ink. God still loves, even if I say, "No."

United Methodist worship resources provide services for reaffirmation of the baptismal covenant. The rubrics for that service are clear about the use of water: "Here water may be used symbolically in ways that cannot be interpreted as baptism, as the pastor says: 'Remember your baptism and be thankful.' "

There is a beauty in having been baptized before one knew what was going on; it is a reminder that God loved me before I knew anything about it (Acts 16:15). There is a beauty in having a renewing spiritual experience after having forgotten God; it is a reminder that the God of my baptism did not let go of me when I tried to let go of God (Acts 10:15). There is a beauty in recalling baptism that was with water from the faucet instead of from the Jordan River; it is a reminder that God's good grace is such that God uses the ordinary things of life to grant the most remarkable gifts of grace (Acts 8:36–38).

United Methodists recognize any baptism that has been done with water and in the name of the Father, the Son, and the Holy Spirit. Although baptism is not required for salvation, it is the ordinary means God uses to incorporate persons into the community of faith. United Methodists accept that baptized members are full members of The United Methodist Church and pray that God's grace will bring such persons to make professions of faith. Such are the gifts of God.

> Enkindle now the heavenly zeal, and make thy mercy known,
> and give our pardoned souls to feel that God and love are one.

Another question: How does baptism equip us for discipleship?

42. What's with all this singing?

Once I was attending a Christian Unity meeting of the North Carolina Council of Churches. We were celebrating the variety of gifts brought by the various denominations and called out what we most appreciated about the denominations represented. When it came time to recognize the valued contribution of United Methodism, most of these Christians from other traditions agreed: it was the music.

We are what we sing. (Will you listen to any radio station, or do you tune primarily to the one playing "your kind of music"?) United Methodists take their singing seriously. Do you want an outline of United Methodist theology? Look at the contents pages of the *UMH* (pp. viii and ix): the hymns are organized by their theological content. Do you want to explore a hymn for its doctrinal place? Look at the top of the page heading for each hymn in the *UMH*: there is (on the left-hand page) a theological category and (on the right-hand page) a subcategory of theological truth. Do you want to grasp more biblical support for teaching? Look at the bottom of each hymn text; many of them have direct scriptural references. Do you want to grow spiritually in your singing? Look at John Wesley's "Directions for Singing" (p. vii of the *UMH*) and note: "Above all sing spiritually. Have an eye to God in every word you sing. Aim at pleasing [God] more than yourself, or any other creature."

Singing is in the United Methodist DNA. Charles Wesley (John's brother, who was also a leader of the burgeoning Methodist movement in eighteenth-century England) wrote over six thousand hymns. Of course, some of them are pretty bad—you cannot write that many without creating a few losers—but his hymns became a primary tool for announcing the good news of free grace, for inviting persons to Christ, and for acknowledging with joy the salvation of souls.

United Methodists have developed hymnals for their diverse family: just for example, *The United Methodist Hymnal* (a congregational worship book); *The Faith We Sing* (additional hymns, including contemporary ones); *Mil Voces Para Celebrar* (Hispanic/Latino hymnal); *Songs of Zion* (African American tradition); *Come, Let Us Sing* (Korean-English edition); *Upper Room Worshipbook* (spiritual formation settings); *Rock of Ages* (retirement communities); *Voices* (Native American heritage); *Hymns from the Four Winds* (Asian American hymnody); *Hymns for Signing* (text of *United Methodist Hymnal* for American Sign Language); and a host of hymns in world languages and traditions.

As John Wesley assured in his comments on Ephesians 5:19

(*Explanatory Notes*), the gift of music will be supplied by the Holy Spirit. So be it.

> Celebrate th'eternal God with harp and psaltery,
> timbrels soft and cymbals loud in this high praise agree;
> praise with every tuneful string; all the reach of heavenly art,
> all the powers of music bring, the music of the heart.

Another question: How has the music of the church shaped what you believe?

8

Bible

 43. What is the Bible's authority?

The Bible's authority comes from God. United Methodists (along with almost all Christian communions) believe that God chose to reveal God's very self by inspiring writers to record accounts of God's movement in, through, and in spite of God's people. The church in prayerful reflection identified those written sources which were consistent with the apostolic faith. For United Methodists, the canon (literally, measuring stick, but here meaning the authorized Scriptures) consists of thirty-nine books of the Old Testament and twenty-seven books of the New Testament. For Christians, Jesus Christ—the Word become flesh (John 1:14)—is the lens through which to look at the Bible.

Although he read voraciously, John Wesley claimed to be "a man of one Book." That view established firm roots for the centrality of Scripture in Methodist life and thought. The Evangelical United Brethren cousins have been no less clear about the Bible: "the true rule and guide for faith and practice" (Confession of Faith, article IV). (See 2 Tim. 3:16.)

The most important thing about the Bible is that it contains all we need to know in order to be saved (article V, Articles of Religion; article IV, Confession of Faith). In effect, the principle is "If it ain't in the Book, don't worry about it, leastways in terms of salvation."

United Methodists do not agree on how to study the Bible (see question 46). Persons might read the same passage and come to diametrically opposed views. Does this mean that one is right and the other wrong? Perhaps, sometimes, it does, but more often it means that God has more to reveal to us than any one of us can grasp (2 Tim. 2:14). In order to hear God, we need each other! Surely the God who inspired poetry (The Psalms), law (Leviticus), history (Exodus), story (Ruth), letters (Romans), Gospels (Matthew), legend (Genesis), admonition (Obadiah), and imagery (Revelation) has recognized that the One Story, One Truth, One Love, One Grace, One Word has many shapes. And all of this just so we can be saved through Jesus Christ!

Come, Holy Ghost (for moved by thee the prophets wrote and spoke), unlock the truth, thyself the key, unseal the sacred book.

Another question: What is the salvation story revealed in the Bible?

44. Why do we call the Bible "God's Word"?

The Bible is God's Word because it contains what God wants to say, what God wants to express, what God seeks to reveal. That Word became flesh and lived among us (John 1:14). An interesting thing about the phrase "lived among us" is that the literal translation of the Greek is "tented among us." With that literal rendition, we get a sense of a tent, a temporary housing that is moved from location to location as needed. God has moved in many ways in many places to speak what needs to be spoken. The Bible, as God's Word, God's speech, is filled with accounts from all kinds of places! God has indeed tented among us, and the Bible is evidence of that (John 21:24–25)!

Distinction should be made between the Bible as "God's Word" and the Bible as "God's words." God's Word is what God has to say to us, but most United Methodists would not assume that the biblical text was dictated word by word for a human writing machine to record. (In fact, this is how Muslims understand God to have revealed the Qur'an [Koran] to the prophet Muhammad; in the Islamic faith, only the Arabic original is the sacred language; the prophet was a passive recipient of the word-for-word text.) John Wesley, who had the highest possible regard for the Scripture, acknowledged that the writings were filtered through human historical context and that the organization of the material—such as chapter divisions—was often done incorrectly ("often separating things that are closely joined, and joining those that are entirely distinct from each other" [preface to *Explanatory Notes*]).

Further, the Articles of Religion aver that Old Testament ceremonies and rites and civil precepts of another time are not binding for the Christian (article VI). (What is binding is obedience to moral teaching.)

No wonder that United Methodists believe that in order to take the Bible seriously, we must study the words in order to hear the Word of God.

Open mine eyes to see thy face, open my heart thyself to know.
And then I through thy Word obtain sure present, and eternal gain.

Another question: What is the essential truth in the Bible?

45. Is the Bible infallible?

Would you like a nice phrase to use when you need to impress your friends? Try "The Bible is soteriologically inerrant." Not only is the sentence impressive, it is also true! "Soteriology"—based on the Greek word *soteria*—is the branch of theology dealing with salvation (see chapter 5). "Inerrant" means "without error." Your new sentence is a way of saying, "The Bible is not mistaken in telling us all we need to know in order to be saved." (See question 43.)

But what about other kinds of errors? This is an important question for United Methodists, and for all Christians who take biblical interpretation as a serious matter. Jesus himself did not have a literal view of Scripture. He interpreted Scripture as having meaning beyond the dictionary meanings of words: "You have heard that it was said to those of ancient times. . . . But I say to you . . ." (Matt. 5:21–22, for example, which moved beyond the literal meaning of Exod. 20:13). Jesus told stories (not literally true) to make a point (the parable of the Prodigal Son in Luke 15:11–32 and the parable of the Rich Fool in Luke 12:16–21, for examples). Jesus quoted Scripture knowing full well that the text was not literally true, but was an image or a metaphor for a truth ("they have shut their eyes," a quotation of Isa. 6:10 in Matt. 13:15, for example).

Does God hear a prayer only if the door is closed (Matt. 6:6)? Does God really shoot people with a bow and arrow (Ps. 64:7)? Is Psalm 25:15 about soccer or about hockey? The Bible is filled with figures of speech that we understand not to be literally true. The Bible is true, but not literally true.

Is the Bible inerrant—without error in terms of science or geography or history? There are United Methodists who believe this to be the case. The Confession of Faith gives a more nuanced understanding of Scripture: "true for faith and practice." This view allows for mistakes in matters other than those related to faith and practice. So, if 2 Samuel 24:9 and 1 Chronicles 21:5 disagree on the number of soldiers in the armies of Israel and Judah, it is of no consequence for faith and practice. So, if 2 Kings 8:26 and 2 Chronicles 22:2 disagree on how old Ahaziah was when he became king, it is of no consequence for faith and practice. (See question 46 on helps for reading the Bible.)

Other United Methodists see the Bible as an infallible book (no human filters) in its original manuscripts. This perspective recognizes the probability of human error in copying, transmitting, and translating the texts given by God. The questions remain: Was God's intent to reveal a book of science or to invite persons to faith? Was God's intent to teach mathematics or to tell how we might be saved? Was God's intent to share geographic facts or to teach us how to live? Faith, salvation, and holy living do not depend on the infallibility of the Bible, only on the truth telling of God, revealed in a number of ways and seen in Jesus Christ.

> Whether the Word be preached or read, no saving benefit I gain
> from empty sounds or letters dead; unprofitable all and vain,
> unless by faith thy word I hear and see its heavenly character.

Another question: In what sense is the Bible true?

46. How do I read the Bible?

John Wesley believed the Bible was twice inspired: once when written and again when read. The same Holy Spirit who brought the Scriptures into being (2 Tim. 3:16) inspires the reader to hear the

Word of God (2 Tim. 3:17). Wesley referred to the Bible as "plain truth for plain people." Its usual meaning is its obvious meaning. We are not to pick and choose among the texts until we find one to our liking! In the preface to his *Explanatory Notes*, Wesley penned, "Every part thereof is worthy of God; and all together are one entire body, wherein is no defect, no excess."

When the Bible is taken as a whole ("one entire body," to use Wesley's term), there is neither too much nor too little. The Bible is a self-balancing act. When texts are pulled out of context or when reading is with a microscope rather than a "macroscope," the biblical witness can be distorted. It is all of a piece.

In an introduction to the 1746 edition of *Standard Sermons*, Wesley outlined his own practice for finding the plain truth of the Bible when there seemed to be conflict or uncertainty. (This is my summary—not Wesley's words.) (1) Find a time and place where interruptions are not likely. (2) Accept the promised presence of the Holy Spirit. (3) Have openness to new places God might lead. (4) Pursue difficult passages by praying, by comparing other biblical texts, by conferring with others in the community of faith, and by drawing on the understandings of the ancient tradition. In this way, Wesley called Methodists to be "worker[s] who [had] no need to be ashamed, rightly explaining the word of truth" (2 Tim. 2:15).

The appropriate clarification of difficult Scripture is other Scripture that is clear. United Methodists are in a tradition that takes the whole Bible seriously (see question 48), so it is valuable, even essential, that any given passage be seen in light of the full revelation of the Bible (Ps. 119:105).

> Come, divine Interpreter, bring me eyes thy book to read,
> ears the mystic words to hear, words which did from thee proceed,
> words that endless bliss impart, kept in an obedient heart.

Another question: What, for you, is the most difficult aspect of reading the Bible?

47. Why do Christians disagree on what the Bible means?

If the Bible is, as Wesley said, "plain truth for plain people," why don't all Christians find the exact same meaning in the biblical text? (I'll let you in on a secret: all United Methodists do not agree on what the Bible means!) Philip William Otterbein writes of "the eternal witness in the Bible." If it is eternal, you'd think we would have figured it all out by now!

But it does not take a very clever observer to recognize the ways that Christians disagree on what the Bible says. Denominations form, dissolve, and form again because we do not agree. (Each of the constituent bodies now in United Methodism has experienced such splintering, some still in place.) Call the roll of issues on which faithful, authentic Christians have disagreed over the centuries: slavery, abortion, homosexuality, role of women, racial segregation, war, labor organization, global warming, economics, and the proper color to use for the Advent paraments!

Three factors drive most of this division: (1) sin, (2) approach to biblical interpretation, and (3) variety of life experience.

1. Paul challenged the church in Corinth to quit squabbling (1 Cor. 1:10). He chalked up divisiveness to persons having worldly wisdom that was foolishness to God (1 Cor. 3:18–19). Human beings ought to know about God because God has shown it to them (Rom. 1:19). God's intent is for all to be saved (Rom. 10:13), but the way we judge one another is a sin, which makes God judge us (Rom. 14:10). Thinking too highly of ourselves is a sin (Rom. 12:3). That sin will sometimes not let us have our minds transformed (Rom. 12:2).

2. United Methodists vary in their approach to biblical interpretation (see questions 3 and 4). If I think God closed down the revelation when the Bible was inspired (not one jot or tittle to be changed—Matt. 5:18–19), then I approach the Bible in one way. If I think God has not finished revealing the meaning of the Scripture (it is a living word—Heb. 4:12), then I approach the Bible in another way.

3. A friend of mine moved to North Carolina from Montana. When he first got here, he said he felt claustrophobic, as if all the

roadside trees and forests of green were closing in on him. In Montana, he had known "big sky" and open land. I, on the other hand, felt right at home with woods and tall pines and roads among towering oaks. These two different ways of "experiencing trees" are simply functions of our life journeys; the places where we stand to do our looking are different from each other. We see the exact same woodland differently. Readers of the Bible bring differing backgrounds, experiences, expectations, hungers, filters, sins, and learning for looking at exactly the same text. God invites us to get past those differences (Gal. 3:28), but until we do, the view is going to be different from person to person.

On what can we agree? Jesus Christ is Lord. Now, let's talk about what that means.

> Join us, in one spirit join, let us still receive of thine;
> still for more on thee we call, thou who fillest all in all.

Another question: What gives you confidence in a biblical interpretation?

48. Why follow the lectionary?

The lectionary is a collection of biblical texts assigned to be read on certain Sundays of the church year or holy days. Many—but by no means all—United Methodist congregations follow this cycle of readings, usually a lesson from the Old Testament, a lesson from an epistle, and a lesson from one of the Gospels. Frequently, they include a selection from the Psalms. The practice of having a portion of the Bible appointed to be read each Sunday goes back at least to the fourth century, if indeed not in previous Jewish custom. The lectionary used by United Methodists was revised in 1992 and follows common readings (on most Sundays) with Roman Catholics, Episcopalians, Presbyterians, Lutherans, and others who value the three-year cycle of readings. (See *BOW*, pp. 227–37.)

Why do this? Following the lectionary leads the preacher away from the temptation of choosing only personal favorite biblical passages. In the course of the three years (cleverly called Year A, Year B, and Year C!), a congregation using the lectionary will hear all the major biblical themes and will explore some texts that otherwise might be hidden. There is a power in the awareness that the congregation where I worship is engaging the same Scriptures as friends in England or Africa or Porthdinllaen, Gwynedd, North Wales. Use of the full lectionary readings will expose a congregation to three or four lessons a Sunday—not bad for a people who hold the Scripture to be foundational!

The use of both Old Testament and New Testament readings helps the church avoid the heresy (false teaching) of Marcion. In the second century, he argued that the Old Testament was no longer valid now that the New Testament was revealed. The Articles of Religion (article VI) speak directly to this issue and declare, "The Old Testament is not contrary to the New."

Some United Methodists feel that following the lectionary binds the Holy Spirit. These persons allow the Spirit to guide the choice of Scripture for preaching. In this freedom, they sense a greater likelihood that the text will be the appropriate word for a given occasion.

Most United Methodist congregations follow the Christian year, giving the thematic and biblical emphases for Advent, Christmas, Epiphany, Lent, Easter, and Pentecost. Often, additional days are observed: All Saints, Christ the King, Ash Wednesday, Maundy Thursday, Good Friday, Transfiguration, Baptism of the Lord, and so forth. Tradition offers colors to be used to reinforce the meaning of the seasons: white, purple, blue, gold, green, black, and red. Clergy vestments vary according to local convention, pastoral preference, and liturgical teaching.

When he first the work begun, small and feeble was his day;
now the Word doth swiftly run, now it wins its widening way;
more and more it spreads and grows, ever mighty to prevail;
sin's strongholds it now o'erthrows, shakes the trembling gates of hell.

Another question: How can the use of the lectionary help or hurt how you hear the gospel?

9

Theology

 49. How do United Methodists do theology?

When I was in seminary, a friend of mine decided to leave The Methodist Church and join another denomination. His district superintendent (see question 76) asked him why. "Well, sir," he replied, "frankly it's because of the Methodist doctrine of the church." "That's nonsense," the superintendent responded. "I've been a Methodist preacher for thirty years and I've never even heard of a doctrine of the church!"

There is some impression among Christians that we United Methodists do a lot things but don't do much theology. But all the "doings" in the United Methodist habit are rooted in biblically based theological thinking. Is it possible that we have led with our doing while hiding our thinking?

If I see someone with red hair, I assume that somewhere in that person's gene pool were the things that make for red hair. When I see United Methodists act in a certain way, I assume there are some things in their theological gene pool that make them act that way. How do we track down that theological gene pool?

There are four standards for testing United Methodist theology (theology means "God word" or "talk about God"). We have touched on each of these in the earlier pages of this book: (1) The Articles of Religion of The Methodist Church—twenty-five statements adapted by John Wesley from the thirty-nine Articles of Religion of the Church of England. (2) The Confession of Faith of the Evangelical United Brethren Church—determined by that denomination on the merger of the Evangelical Church and the United Brethren Church. (There are common theological roots intertwining these historically German-speaking groups with the primarily English-speaking Methodists. The Articles and the Confession were deemed "congruent" when EUBs and Methodists merged in 1968.) (3) *Standard Sermons of John Wesley*—teachings done by Wesley in a sermon format. (4) *Explanatory Notes upon the New Testament*, by John Wesley—in which Wesley translates and comments on the New Testament revelation.

Restrictive rules in the United Methodist Constitution say that the General Conference "shall not revoke, alter, or change [these documents] or establish any new standards or rules of doctrine contrary to our present existing and established standards of doctrine." United Methodists take theology seriously!

United Methodists use four guidelines when doing theology. These four are sometimes called the Wesley quadrilateral, although John Wesley never used the term. Of these four, Scripture is primary. The other three are tradition, reason, and experience. These dimensions "talk to one another," with Scripture given primacy. Because these guidelines "talk" to one another, one writer has preferred the term "quadrilogical," suggesting "four words" or a "four-way conversation," rather than "quadrilateral" or "four sides."

The Book of Discipline says that Scripture reveals the Word of God (Eph. 6:17); tradition is a source and measure of Christian witness (Heb. 12:1); human experience confirms the biblical story (1 John 1:1); reason relates Scripture to wider knowledge (Isa. 1:18).

> Ye servants of God, your Master proclaim,
> and publish abroad his wonderful name;
> the name all-victorious of Jesus extol,
> his kingdom is glorious and rules over all.

Another question: In what ways are you a theologian?

5O. Are United Methodists liberal or conservative?

There are conservative United Methodists and there are liberal United Methodists; there are folks in the middle and folks off the charts at both extremes. "Liberal" and "conservative" are shorthand terms we have for either pigeonholing people or quickly finding compatriots for the struggles of church life.

Some United Methodists say, "I am a conservative in matters of theology and a liberal in matters of social policy." Others might proclaim, "I am liberal in my view of Scripture, but my conclusions are socially conservative." Or, "I am so conservative that I will only get out of bed on the right side." Or, "I am so liberal that I only shake hands with my left hand."

Members of some denominations portray all United Methodists as liberals. Some members of other denominations think of United Methodists as hopelessly behind the times. Why is it so important to label one another? John Wesley counseled Christians of catholic (universal) spirit to show love to all. "Do you show your love by your works? While you have time, as you have opportunity, do you in fact 'do good to all'—neighbors or strangers, friends or enemies, good or bad? Do you do them all the good you can?" (*Works*, vol. 2, p. 89).

If we put descriptors on one another in order to direct and redirect our love, we have failed a basic scriptural principle (1 Cor. 13:13; 1 John 2:10–11). Love is impartial. Perfect love (there's that word "perfect" again—see question 23) casts out the fear we have of one another (1 John 4:16–21).

What makes someone conservative? Is it the desire to conserve things of great value? What makes someone liberal? Is it the desire to free all for joyful obedience? Frankly, I'd like a dose of each. We need each other to bring the gift of balance that God seems to have given United Methodism. We balance faith and works. We balance justification and sanctification. We balance Word and sacrament. We balance personal holiness and social holiness. We balance liturgical worship and revival spirit. We balance personal piety and social justice. Could "liberal" and "conservative" be another balancing ministry to which God calls us?

> His only righteousness I show, his saving truth proclaim;
> 'tis all my business here below to cry, "Behold the Lamb!"

Another question: Do you think United Methodism is liberal or conservative or . . . ?

51. Why be concerned about theology?

United Methodists are concerned about theology because theology puts into focus our relationship with God. There are numerous strands of theology: biblical theology, systematic theology, liberation theology, philosophical theology, apocalyptic theology, ecological theology, feminist theology, black theology, process theology, gay theology, neoorthodox theology, postmodern theology, existential theology, holiness theology, womanist theology, mystical theology, narrative theology, men's theology, empirical theology—surely you can find one in that list that you like!

To that bountiful inventory, United Methodists might add another: practical theology. John Wesley used the term "practical divinity." We are concerned about theology because our theology shapes how we live our lives. If one's theology does not transform one's life, that theology must be out of touch with the transforming God revealed in Jesus Christ! United Methodist tradition is less about abstract theological thought and more about life-changing theological reflection and declaration.

In sum, the United Methodist practical theology is that life is different because God is seeking to love us; after all, Zacchaeus's life changed when God's love found him (Luke 19:1–10). Then, we love because we have first been loved (1 John 4:19). United Methodists are clear that love is not lonely; it finds social expression. (It finds expression in relationships, in social justice, in dialogue.) In *The United Methodist Hymnal*, one of the headings for hymns draws on this traditional Wesleyan terminology: Social Holiness (hymns 425–450).

One of the memorable stories in United Methodist history recounts that Philip William Otterbein greeted Martin Boehm with the powerful words *Wir sind Brüder*—"We are brethren!" That social nature of religion grew out of theological perception that ultimately saw persons as brothers and sisters. It is no wonder, no coincidence, that United Methodist people have established Social Principles, formal statements adopted by the General Conference (see question 74) to express the practical implications of responding to the call to love everyone. After all, God's prevenient grace has been given everyone, so let the grace in me meet the grace in you! The Social Principles (and a companion *Book of Resolutions*) address topics as wide-ranging as sexuality, immigration, war, gambling, ecology, aging, racism, divorce, harassment, rural life, AIDS, suicide, tobacco, alcohol, poverty, capital punishment, genetic research, and property rights. That's a sample, not complete, list!

United Methodist action (practical divinity) is an expression of a theology of grace, a practice of love, and a commitment to share a glimpse of the coming reign of God. That's why theology is important.

> Come, thou long-expected Jesus, born to set thy people free;
> from our fears and sins release us, let us find our rest in thee.
> Israel's strength and consolation, hope of all the earth thou art;
> dear desire of every nation, joy of every longing heart.

Another question: What is the difference between "doing good" and "Christian love"?

52. Why is education so important to United Methodists?

Around the world, there are over seven hundred educational institutions related to The United Methodist Church. Whether it is a seminary in Moscow, Russia, or a university in Harare, Zimbabwe, or Ewha Womans University in Seoul, South Korea, or Ganta Elementary School in Liberia, or one of the one hundred twenty-three United Methodist schools in the United States, United Methodists have a strong investment in ministries of education.

Why not? The Methodist movement began on a university campus in England (Oxford). Philip William Otterbein was a university professor before he was a pastor. The organizing conference of the Methodist Episcopal Church in America in 1784 voted to establish a college. John Wesley supported Kingswood School to provide education for the children of his preachers. The oldest two-year church-related college in the United States is a United Methodist institution, Louisburg College. The world's oldest college for women is a United Methodist school, Wesleyan College in Macon, Georgia. There are thirteen United Methodist schools of theology and about seventy other seminaries approved for United Methodist theological education.

United Methodists hear God's call to love God with heart and mind (Matt. 22:37). Truth is of God (John 8:31–32), so there is no reason to fear the search for truth. Charles Wesley wrote a hymn that, sadly, is no longer in the official hymnal of United Methodism: for the dedication of Kingswood School, he wrote, "Unite the pair so long disjoined, Knowledge and vital piety; Learning and holiness combined, And truth and love, let all men see In these whom up to thee we give, Thine, wholly thine, to die and live." That unity of holy living and learning is the goal of United Methodist involvement in education. (The motto of Duke University, a United Methodist school, is "Eruditio et Religio," variously translated as "knowledge and faith" or "education and religion.")

The United Methodist Church has educational requirements for its clergy. Those who do not have a master's degree from an approved seminary (which most do) have to complete a minimum of a five-year part-time Course of Study. (Those seeking to become full members of the annual conference also need an additional thirty-two hours of graduate theological education.) This is in the tradition of the apostle Paul, who was educated at the feet of the scholar Gamaliel (Acts 22:3) and after his conversion spent time learning of the faith from others (Acts 9:19).

With this emphasis on education, it is not surprising that each week almost two million United Methodists gather in local churches for extensive Sunday school curriculum. Others meet during the week in various study settings. Education is important because it helps us offer our best minds and thoughts to God.

> I want the witness, Lord, that all I do is right,
> according to thy mind and word, well-pleasing in thy sight.

Another question: How well do education and faith mix?

 ### 53. How does United Methodist theology differ from other theologies?

If theologies could be put on a pair of hanging scales, United Methodist theology would be close to balance with other Protestant

Christian traditions. There are points of emphasis and heritage, but the central belief in the saving Lordship of Jesus Christ is the same. Jesus prayed that his people might be one (John 17:11). That prayer was framed in reference to the Trinity (John 17:11—"as we are one"). The tragedy of the divided church is that it distorts the image of the Trinity, three persons in one community.

As a worldwide body, United Methodists vary in theological emphasis from place to place. Although the core doctrine is the same, the accent may shift locally. Forms of worship, styles of leadership, and identified moral issues will ebb and flow, but the driving passion among United Methodists is always the encounter of the grace of God with the human condition.

Denominations sometimes differ from each other in ethos (generally, the socioeconomic makeup of congregations; the diversity within membership; the culture of food; social practices; historic values; degrees of formality; generational stories). Even though these differences might actually be more divisive than theology, there are varying denominational theological tones.

In The Episcopal Church, for example, clergy are understood to be in an apostolic succession of sequential laying on of hands by authorized bishops. In United Methodism, that is the normative practice, but John Wesley understood himself (as a priest in the Church of England) to have the same authority as a New Testament bishop and did what might be called "extraordinary ordinations."

Lutherans and United Methodists diverge on how to understand the nature of Christ's presence at the Lord's Supper.

The classic distinctions between Presbyterians and United Methodists center in the theology of predestination and its cohort teaching of election. The nature of human free will is also an issue, as is the doctrine of Christian perfection.

Baptists practice believer's baptism only. United Methodists observe both believer's baptism and infant baptism. (Infant baptism is the dominant Christian practice around the world, including Roman Catholic, Orthodox, Anglican, Lutheran, and most Reformed traditions such as Presbyterian.) Some Baptist traditions will accept as valid only baptism by immersion; United Methodists acknowledge three modes of baptism: immersion, pouring, and, most commonly, sprinkling.

Church government and polity vary among denominations. The biggest contrast is between congregationally governed denominations (such as United Church of Christ) and connectionally organized denominations (such as United Methodist). For United Methodists, decision making rests in a series of conferences (see question 74).

In contrast to some other polities (Presbyterian and Baptist, for example), United Methodism has bishops for particular ministries of superintending; they are a sign of the unity of the church and supervise the whole church. (Incidentally, John Wesley preferred that this office be referred to as "general superintendent," rather than "bishop.")

Why would God allow all these variations to exist? Maybe God has more to give than will fit into any one basket! In order for none of God's gifts to be lost, each denomination needs to understand and to offer what God has put into its basket. "Like good stewards of the manifold grace of God, serve one another with whatever gift each of you has received" (1 Pet. 4:10).

> To serve the present age, my calling to fulfill;
> O may it all my powers engage to do my Master's will!

Another question: How does God use denominational differences?

 ## 54. Why are United Methodists so exercised about homosexuality?

The United Methodist Church, like most denominations in the United States, is not of one mind on the subject of homosexuality. Is a homosexual orientation an aberration in God's created order? Is homosexual practice sinful? Is homosexuality one of God's good gifts of sexuality? Should homosexual persons serve in ordained ministry? How should local congregations relate to homosexuals who wish to be members? What civil rights should homosexual couples have? What does it mean for homosexuals, no less than heterosexuals, to have sacred worth?

If Scripture is primary in matters of faith and practice, then care must be given to exploring the biblical texts that seem, at some level at least, to reference homosexuality. These texts are usually identified as

Genesis 19:1–29; Leviticus 18:1–30; Leviticus 20:1–27; Judges 19:22–30; Romans 1:24–27; 1 Corinthians 6:9–17; 1 Timothy 1:6–11; and Jude 5–7. (Some scholars think some of these passages have nothing to do with homosexuality.) Students of the Bible note that the Gospels are silent on anything Jesus might have said on the subject.

Immediately, the lines are drawn as faithful persons disagree on how the Bible is to be studied (see question 47). What is the nature of biblical authority (see question 43)? How do these verses fit into the overarching message of the Word (see question 4)? How do we relate new scientific and psychological insights to the understandings of biblical writers? What does human experience (see question 49) confirm about biblical truth? Which threads of church tradition are most helpful in hearing what God would say?

A rather unfortunate image comes to my mind: United Methodists hitting each other over the head with a Bible. (I hope they are all editions with soft covers!) The good news is that all United Methodists seem to be taking the Bible seriously. The bad news is that we are hearing all sorts of variations on the message. There is, nevertheless, something healthy about Christians searching the Bible together for a revelation of God's will for God's creation. United Methodists from multiple perspectives are exercised about homosexuality because they take the Bible seriously, because they think all persons have sacred worth, and because they care for holy living.

Sad to say, some of the extreme energy in the debate about homosexuality comes from (a) a few persons who fear any sexual expression other than their own, and (b) some persons who assume the worst about anyone who disagrees with their own view of sexuality. Although these edges are rare in United Methodism, they do provide fuel for fires that keep others from finding good ways to hear and learn from each other. A trust in the good intentions of those with whom we disagree can go a long way toward allowing us to hear one another (Acts 10:28).

> What troubles have we seen, what mighty conflicts past,
> fightings without, and fears within, since we assembled last!
> Yet out of all the Lord hath brought us by his love;
> and still he doth his help afford, and hides our life above.

Another question: What are the core biblical revelations about sexuality?

10

Christian Life

55. What are the means of grace?

Early in the ministry of John Wesley, he had a controversy with Moravians, who argued that there was nothing a person could do to get God's grace other than simply waiting for it. Wesley called this Moravian view "quietism." Wesley thought we were not just to wait for God, but that we were to access the means God had chosen to give us grace. In a sermon based on Malachi 3:7 ("You have turned aside from my statutes and have not kept them"), Wesley spelled out the means that God ordinarily uses to give grace to humankind. Grace still comes as a gift—not automatically—because "all outward means whatever, if separate from the Spirit of God, cannot profit at all" (*Works*, vol. 1, p. 382). God can give grace through any channel or experience as God chooses, but United Methodists continue to recognize that in the common experience of the church, there are means through which God ordinarily gives grace.

In this sermon, Wesley named the chief means of grace: both private and public prayer (1 Thess. 5:17); searching the Scripture: reading, hearing, meditating (2 Tim. 3:16–17); and the Lord's Supper (1 Cor. 11:23–26). In the General Rules (the guide for early Methodist societies), Wesley expanded the list to add the public worship of God (1 Cor. 14:26) and fasting or abstinence (Matt. 6:17–18). The early Methodist, United Brethren, and Evangelical (see question 67) prominence of small groups and the regular meetings for conference led to the inclusion of holy conferencing as a means of grace (Acts 15:6). (Baptism is not included, probably because it is not a repeated act. See question 41.)

United Methodists acknowledge two categories of the means of

(internal)

grace: (1) works of piety—also called instituted means of grace, such as those named in the paragraph above, and (2) works of mercy *(external)* also called prudential means of grace, such as those to which our Lord invites us in Matthew 25:31–46: feeding the hungry, welcoming the stranger, caring for the sick, and visiting the prisoner. To be among the poor, the hungry, the sick, the imprisoned is a means of grace for us! In typical Wesleyan fashion, there is a balance between divine initiative and human action. Grace is still God's to give (or not, as God chooses), but United Methodists celebrate and practice the means by which God ordinarily gives such grace.

> Plenteous grace with thee is found, grace to cover all my sin;
> let the healing streams abound, make and keep me pure within.
> Thou of life the fountain art, freely let me take of thee;
> Spring thou up within my heart; rise to all eternity.

Another question: Which means of grace is the most difficult for you to practice?

56. What are works of mercy?

Early Methodists in America spoke of "spreading scriptural holiness over the land." Jacob Albright, founder of the movement that led to the Evangelical Church flow in The United Methodist Church, got into trouble with some of his Lutheran, Reformed, and Mennonite neighbors because he insisted that salvation not only involved ritual but meant a change of heart, a different way of living. Records show that Christian Newcomer, an early leader among the United Brethren, once bought a slave girl and included in the bill of sale provisions for her release to freedom. What do all of these strands of United Methodism have in common?

The mutual theme is that "scriptural holiness" is more than personal piety. Scriptural holiness means that life and all its relationships are now shaped by the love of God and love of neighbor (Matt. 22:36–40). John Wesley wrote, "Christianity is essentially a social religion and . . . to turn it into a solitary religion is indeed to destroy it" (*Works*, vol. 1, p. 533). Out of this context, Wesley taught that God blessed with grace those works of mercy which extended the gospel as love of neighbor (Jas. 2:14–26). (See question 55 for a reflection on works of piety and works of mercy.)

When United Methodists are careful about understanding their busy lives of service, they see that these "works of mercy" are gifts of God's sanctifying grace (see question 25). The classic term "entire sanctification" (see question 23) includes full love of neighbor. Deeds of love are possible because of God's grace and deeds of love are a means of God's grace.

United Methodists do not always agree with one another about the best way to offer healing, justice, caring, feeding, visiting, welcoming, and the other acts of mercy. Those differences can be summarized by simply listing some American political figures who are United Methodists: Hillary Rodham Clinton, George W. Bush, Dick Cheney, John Edwards, Dennis Hastert, George McGovern, and, from the past, George Wallace, Terry Sanford, and Shirley Chisholm. (Wouldn't that make for an interesting room filled with "holy conferencing"!)

This wide United Methodist concern for neighbor grows out of a conviction that God seeks to reconcile all things to God's very self (Col. 1:20). Whether it is chicken soup taken to a sick friend, an appeal to a state legislature not to begin a lottery, a counseling service for persons considering abortion, a thinking-of-you card to a lonely neighbor, a work team replacing a roof after Hurricane Katrina, a meal served at an urban soup kitchen, a smile for someone who comes to church dressed differently, standing in line to vote, or knitting a shawl as a gift for an ill child, United Methodists join countless other Christians in works of mercy. Otherwise, in the words of John Wesley, we have "dead, imaginary faith."

For thee delightfully employ whate'er thy bounteous grace hath given; and run my course with even joy, and closely walk with thee to heaven.

Another question: What is the relationship between faith and good works?

57. What about prayer?

In reflecting on 1 Thessalonians 5:16–17 in his *Explanatory Notes*, John Wesley referred to prayer as "the breath of our spiritual life." No one lives without breathing; there is no life in the Spirit without prayer. In enjoining the Thessalonians to constant prayer, Paul chose the word *adialĕiptŏs*, which literally means "permanent" or "without ever being absent." Prayer understood in this way is more than the use of words or intentional time and place. It is an attitude of full openness to God. My love of my wife is constant; I always have an attitude of loving her, but it surely doesn't hurt to find ways to tell her every so often! Prayer carries that same kind of rhythm of spoken and unspoken communication.

God answers prayer. Such is the witness of the Gospels (Matt. 7:7–11; 21:22; Mark 11:24; Luke 11:9; John 11:22). Such is the witness of the early church (2 Cor. 1:11; Jas. 5:16; Rev. 5:8). Such is the witness of our ancestors in the faith. Such is our own journey of trust.

In his sermon on "The Means of Grace," John Wesley preached "All who desire the grace of God are to wait for it in the way of prayer." United Methodists have not thought that the one who prays can demand or predict how God is to answer a prayer. In fact, Romans 8:26–27 alerts us to the reality that even our best praying falls short, and God's Spirit has to go to bat for us according to the will of God. Prayer is a discipline of honesty before God and openness to God. Praying "in Jesus' name" makes our intent clear to pray in the manner, spirit, and power of Jesus.

United Methodists, both in private prayer and in public prayer, often draw on written or memorized prayers prepared for the occasion, but more frequently on those of the ancient and historic church. This practice creates a marvelous community of prayer, reaching across time and space, uniting us with saints who have gone before us (Rev. 5:8). Congregational unison prayers give verbal expression to that community. The most common corporate prayer is the one our Lord taught (Matt. 6:9–13). In that prayer, Jesus modeled conversation with God that reflected praise, daily life, and submission to God's will. There is a splendid mystery about how (and when) God answers prayer. It must be one of the ways God has to keep life from getting boring!

Jesus, confirm my heart's desire to work and speak and think for thee; still let me guard the holy fire, and still stir up thy gift in me.

Another question: Why do you say that God does (or does not) listen to all prayers?

58. What about healing?

About twenty minutes from where I live is the Duke Medical Center. It is a mammoth facility devoted to the full range of healing arts. It is part of Duke University, a United Methodist institution.

Twelve miles from my home is a place where faithful Christians gather every Tuesday night to pray for sick people, to help them get well. It is a United Methodist congregation.

A few years back, when I had surgery, I received in the mail a prayer cloth from persons who said they had prayed over that fabric, asking God to heal me. They were in a United Methodist church.

Last week, a nearby congregation invited people to come for the laying on of hands and anointing with oil for healing. It was a United Methodist gathering.

A couple of months ago, I read of a woman who carried her sick child to a faith-healing service where the promise was made that faith would heal. She was United Methodist.

United Methodists employ numerous ways to be in touch with God's gift of healing (1 Cor. 12:9; Luke 7:21). Most frequently, the power of health comes through the ministry of the medical community, but God's expansive grace is such that there are witnesses to cures beyond the logic of science. In either case, it is God who heals (Ps. 147:3; Prov. 4:22).

John Wesley so valued the wholeness of persons, including their physical well-being, that he produced a book of remedies (*The Primitive Physick: An Easy and Natural Method of Curing Most Diseases*) so medical care would be available to the poor. United Methodists seek for a glimpse of that coming reign of God in which there is no sickness (Rev. 22:2).

Most of us do not have a problem accepting God's will when health is restored. But then, people die. People linger in pain. People lose mental and social faculties. What has gone wrong? Is God punishing them? (Jesus did not think so—John 9:2–3). Is their faith inadequate? (Jesus died in spite of his faith—Mark 14:36). We all share in the fallenness of creation (Rom. 8:22–23), and our illnesses and death mirror that. That doesn't make it God's will. Disease is not because I am personally bad, but because I'm human. (Of course, bad personal lifestyle choices impact our health; we understand that. The question is, rather, about the apparent non sequitur nature of some diseases.)

God heals even when God does not cure. In the New Testament, the word used most frequently for "healing" is *thĕrapĕnō*, a word that has the same root as "attendant." United Methodists understand that healing is that attending presence of God, a love from which nothing can separate us (Rom. 8:38–39). It might not look like what we expected or for which we hoped, but nothing separates us from that healing presence.

> Thou, O Christ, art all I want, more than all in thee I find;
> raise the fallen, cheer the faint, heal the sick, and lead the blind.

Another question: What would lead you to say someone is healed?

59. Why be involved in justice?

"To do righteousness and justice is more acceptable to the LORD than sacrifice" (Prov. 21:3).

"But let justice roll down like waters, and righteousness like an everflowing stream" (Amos 5:24).

"What does the LORD require of you but to do justice, and to love kindness, and to walk humbly with your God?" (Mic. 6:8.)

"For God shows no partiality" (Rom. 2:11).

"But be doers of the word, and not merely hearers who deceive themselves" (Jas. 1:22).

As a people who seek to be biblical in character, United Methodists are engaged in works for justice. Such ministry is God's vision for the sanctification of the whole world (Col. 1:20). Over the years, there have been times when United Methodist people (and their predecessors) have failed miserably in that mission. The Salvation Army split from English Methodism because some felt the Methodists had lost passion for the "least and the lost." In 1844, the Methodist Episcopal Church broke into two separate denominations, one that made room for slavery and one that worked against slavery. In 1939, three branches of Methodism reunited to form The Methodist Church, but with the price of segregating black members into their own separate administrative jurisdiction. In the Evangelical Association, an argument over the right way to have a mission in Japan expanded into attacks and counterattacks, resulting in a thirty-year division in that part of the family. Dare I say, "Etc., etc."?

But when at their best, United Methodist people have thrown full strength into efforts to bring justice and right relations into the world. The last letter John Wesley wrote was to William Wilberforce, imploring that member of the British Parliament to lead the fight against slavery, which Wesley called "the scandal of religion" and "the vilest that ever saw the sun." Otterbein worked to relieve poverty wherever he lived. The 1908 Methodist Episcopal Church adopted a Social Creed, an endeavor aimed at sensitizing Methodists to places in the world where there were hurts to be healed, peace to be sought, equal rights to be gained, social evils to be fought, and prophetic witness to be made. Denominational agencies (now known as the General Board of Church and Society) were put into place to give resources and vision for the task of joining God in the mission of bringing justice and righteousness. Generally, United Methodist official positions (as expressed by the General Conference—see question 74) define justice in these ways: war, against it; racism, against it; sexual harassment, against it; protection of environment, for it; gender discrimination, against it; health care, for everyone; abortion: regrettable, but never for birth control; religious minorities, have rights; homosexuality, practice incompatible with Christian teaching; affirmative action, for it; sexual orientation, have rights; alcohol, support abstinence; tobacco, recommend abstinence; human cloning, oppose it; private property, trusteeship from God; gambling, oppose it; death penalty, oppose it; military service, support those who do and those who don't; United Nations, endorse it.

Please realize that this summary (based on the actions of the 2004 General Conference) only hits high spots from 30 pages of Social Principles and 954 pages of resolutions. Those figures alone, plus the visibility of United Methodist witness, reflect an ongoing effort to take seriously the biblical call for personal holiness and social justice.

O might the universal Friend this havoc of his creatures see!
Bid our unnatural discord end, declare us reconciled in thee!
Write kindness on our inward parts and chase the murderer from our
    hearts!

Another question: If sin prevents justice from full blossom in this life, why even bother to seek justice?

60. Why does it make a difference how I live my life?

How I live my life is important because how I live my life reflects my relationship with Jesus Christ. For all of the value given to community and connection (see questions 2, 19, 31, 36, 37, 46, 55), United Methodists assert that a personal relationship with Jesus Christ is essential (Luke 7:50; John 5:34; Acts 16:30; 1 Tim. 2:4).

The acceptance of Jesus Christ as Savior is inescapably personal. There is a clue in the way we baptize: the person being baptized is called by name; it is no generic gift of grace—it is the claim of God on this individual life. The questions asked in the service of profession of faith (*UMH*, pp. 46–47, for example) are to be answered in the first person singular: "Do you truly and earnestly repent of your sins?" "I do." Although one rejoices in the community of faith and love that has brought him or her to this stage of the journey, the profession one makes is individual and personal. The liturgical act of laying on of hands in confirmation or reaffirmation is accompanied by the calling of the name of the individual: "John Mark, the Lord defend you with his heavenly grace . . ."

United Methodist heritage turns as metal filings toward a magnet as the Bible offers its clear testimony to the difference that Jesus Christ makes in a life: "Once you were not a people, but now you are God's people" (1 Pet. 2:10); "Go your way, and from now on do not sin again" (John 8:11); "Do not be overcome by evil, but overcome evil with good" (Rom. 12:21); "Try to find out what is pleasing to the Lord" (Eph. 5:10); "I regard everything as loss because of the surpassing value of knowing Christ Jesus my Lord" (Phil. 3:8); "Put to death, therefore, whatever in you is earthly" (Col. 3:5). The transformed life in Christ Jesus provides the blood that courses through the veins of United Methodism.

Sometimes we miss the mark (see question 65). But the goal of the holy life ("going on to perfection"—see question 23) moves the justified Christian inexorably toward sanctification (see question

25). It is that path toward holiness that makes a difference in how we live.

(1) Personal morality—my speech, my stewardship, my use of time, my avoidance of gambling, my purity of thought—grows out of Jesus' love for me, my acceptance of that love, and the grace that makes it all possible. (2) Social morality—my work for justice (see question 59), my concern for neighbor, my demand for human equality, my passion for peace, my hunger for reconciliation—grows out of Jesus' love for me, my acceptance of that love, and the grace that makes it all possible. That's why it makes a difference in how I live my life.

I want a principle within of watchful, godly fear,
a sensibility of sin, a pain to feel it near.
I want the first approach to feel of pride or wrong desire,
To catch the wandering of my will, and quench the kindling fire.

Another question: What connection is there between happiness and holiness?

11

Reign of God

 61. What and where is the kingdom of God?

The kingdom of God is the reign of God and is anywhere God's victory is totally won. Jesus testified that the triumph of God (also called "the kingdom of heaven") was at hand (Matt. 4:17). Our Lord taught disciples to pray, "Your kingdom come. Your will be done, on earth as it is in heaven" (Matt. 6:10). The disciples are told that the first thing to do is to strive after that reign of God (Matt. 6:33). Jesus told a lot of stories about what that kingdom would be like: weeds to be destroyed, wheat to be kept (Matt. 13:24–30); tiny mustard seed that grows to be a great bush (Matt. 13:31–32); rich people having a hard time getting in (Mark 10:23–27); poor to have a place (Luke 6:20); anticipation of a great banquet (Luke 22:18). One can almost open the Gospels at random and find some image, some forecast, some announcement of the kingdom. And the kingdom does not look like business as usual! The values and systems of the world are turned upside down.

Over the years, scholars have debated whether the kingdom is here or is partially here or is yet to come. All of those answers seem to be true! Pharisees once asked Jesus when the kingdom of God would arrive. Our Lord cautioned, "Don't be looking for signs. The truth of the matter is that the kingdom is among you" (Luke 17:20–21). Or an alternate translation says, "the kingdom is inside you." The kingdom is now.

Yet, John Wesley writes that when we pray the Lord's Prayer we are praying: "May Thy kingdom of grace come quickly, and swallow up all the kingdoms of the earth!" (*Explanatory Notes*, Matt. 6:10). That hasn't happened yet. The kingdom is still to come.

And yet, Jesus expected the reign of God within a generation (Mark 9:1). John Wesley says that happened at Pentecost, when the Holy Spirit poured out power on the gathered disciples (Acts 2:1–4). The kingdom is partially here.

The net result of these various biblical references to the kingdom is a conclusion that the kingdom's life could be seen in Jesus Christ, that even now in the twenty-first century we get glimpses of God's reign, and that in a time that seems good to God, the full reign of God will restore a future that we have already seen in Christ. Death and evil will not only have lost their power, but will be destroyed. "Your throne, O God, is forever and ever" (Heb. 1:8; Ps. 45:6).

> Rejoice, the Lord is King! Your Lord and King adore;
> mortals, give thanks and sing, and triumph evermore. . . .
> His kingdom cannot fail, he rules o'er earth and heaven;
> The keys of earth and hell are to our Jesus given.
> Lift up your heart, lift up your voice; rejoice; again I say,
> rejoice.

Another question: Where have you gotten glimpses of God's kingdom?

62. Why is what I think about the future important?

Next week, I am driving to Lake Junaluska, so I have to get my car serviced in the next couple of days.

Nephew Robby and his wife, Iris, are coming to visit us for a few days, so there is some straightening up we need to do around the house.

The deadline for the manuscript for this book is soon and very soon, so I had best stick to this writing!

That's the way life unfolds. What I do today is shaped by what I see in the future. We who want to live our lives "no longer by human desires but by the will of God" (1 Pet. 4:2) make our plans for today based on the future that we see God unfolding (see question 61). If

God is putting together a world in which love is going to be the "life principle," I had best get with the program! Now!

When Martin Boehm was chosen (by lot, which was the Mennonite custom) to be the minister for his local congregation, he was horrified. His total life had been as a quiet farmer, and he felt ill prepared to exhort the faithful; but his future was clear: he was to serve as a minister. Seeing that future, he set about preparing himself for the task, chiefly by fervent prayer and fresh surrender. In the agony of those days, he even felt himself spiritually lost. He cried out, "Lost! Lost!" He heard the voice of his Master: "I am come to seek and save that which was lost" (Luke 19:10 KJV). Because Martin Boehm got a glimpse of his future, he had a different spiritual journey for his present. (His ministry was a key ingredient in the planting of the United Brethren seeds for the United Methodist tree.)

United Methodists engage in social actions of compassion and justice now (see question 59) because there is a future when God's reign will be compassion and justice (Eph. 1:10). United Methodists give a central place to worship now (see question 37) because there is a future when God's reign will find the saints gathered at the throne of God to offer praise (Rev. 4:10–11). United Methodists practice hospitality and invitation to the gospel now (see question 30) because there is a future when God's reign will say to all who are thirsty, "Come! The water of life is free!" (Rev. 22:17).

Yea, Amen! Let all adore thee, high on thy eternal throne;
Savior, take the power and glory, claim the kingdom for thine own.
Hallelujah! Hallelujah! Hallelujah! Everlasting God, come down!

Another question: What is the future God wants to give?

63. What is the nature of heaven?

One of John Wesley's most focused statements comes in the preface to a collection of his sermons: "I want to know one thing, the way to heaven—how to land safe on that happy shore. God himself has condescended to teach the way: for this very end he came from heaven" (*Works*, vol. 1, p. 105).

In a sermon attacking predestination (see question 30), John Wesley spells out his understanding of the route to heaven: "(1) God knows all believers; (2) wills that they should be saved from sin; (3) to that end justifies them; (4) sanctifies; and (5) takes them to glory" (*Works*, vol. 2, p. 421).

The Apostles' Creed speaks of "the life everlasting." The Nicene Creed speaks of "the life of the world to come." United Methodists join with the wider Christian family to affirm that God offers joyful, complete, eternal fellowship with Christ and with the saints who share that victory of faith. Jesus teaches us to pray to "our Father in heaven" (Matt. 6:9). John writes that what he records in the book of Revelation is a vision inside the open door of heaven (Rev. 4:4). Within the limits of human speech, it is easiest to think of heaven as a place (Rev. 2:7; 22:14); biblical imagery also seems to think of heaven as a relationship (1 Cor. 15:50; Eph. 1:3). Heaven is seen in relational terms ("the city" [Rev. 22:14]; a "banquet" [Matt. 22:1–14]; a "covenant" [Heb. 9:15]; a shared meal [Luke 22:14–16]). (The fellowship meal at the Lord's Table is an appetizer for heaven [see questions 38, 39]!)

After feeling grace as prevenient, justifying, and sanctifying grace (see question 25), the believer knows grace as glorifying grace (Phil. 3:21). Admission to heaven is by grace through faith (Eph. 2:8). "You can't take it with you" means wealth, power, position, and even good works will not be sufficient for eternal salvation (Gal. 2:16). God through Jesus Christ judges us (Rom. 2:16; 14:12; Matt. 12:36, for example). The standard is the perfect love (see question 23) to which we are called (1 John 4:17). It is the merit of Jesus' perfect love applied to us that saves us (1 John 5:11–12).

One of John Wesley's favorite texts was Eph. 2:8 ("For by grace you have been saved through faith"). Wesley loved to point out that the language was in the past tense; it is a salvation already accomplished in Christ and obtained by faith. Heaven is that full presence of God which has already begun! And because the mortal can put on immortality (literally, as we would put on new clothes—1 Cor. 15:54), the journey continues in a new heaven (Rev. 21:1).

> Let us for this faith contend, sure salvation is the end;
> heaven already is begun, everlasting life is won.

Another question: What do you want heaven to be like?

64. What is the nature of hell?

If heaven is eternal fellowship with God, then hell is the absence of that fellowship. The Confession of Faith (article XII) settles on the term "endless condemnation." John Wesley has an intriguing note in his reflection on Hebrews 9:27: "At the moment of death, every man's final state is determined. But there is not a word in Scripture of a particular judgment immediately after death" (*Explanatory Notes*). Wesley is sure there is a judgment, but he is not so sure that it is implemented right after a person dies. (It is as if Wesley says we are in a "holding pattern" after death until the final Day of Judgment, when God's kingdom is fully established. It makes me feel better to recognize that even the giants in the faith were not transparently clear about some of these mysteries!)

Whereas the traditional language of the Apostles' Creed declared that Jesus "descended into hell," more recent versions say that Jesus "descended to the dead." Both wordings mean the same thing: Jesus gave a chance of salvation to those who lived before his earthly ministry (1 Pet. 3:19–20; 4:6). Wesley left out this phrase when he amended the Articles of Religion, and, accordingly, most United Methodist usage of the Apostles' Creed omits "he descended to the dead." (Contrast the creed in the *UMH* on p. 41 and number 882 with the version at *UMH* 881.)

Admission into early Methodist societies was on the basis of a "desire to flee the wrath to come." The images of fire and brimstone (Matt. 25:41; Rev. 21:8) show the efforts of human language to describe a brokenness, an emptiness, that is beyond the range of our language. If I were to say that "I'm going to beat the stuffing out of you," you would get my message even though you did not anticipate your insides actually pouring out onto the sidewalk. In the same manner, Jesus often used an everyday image to communicate with people; he referred to the place of punishment as *gehenna* (which we translate as hell—Matt. 5:22; 18:9; Luke 12:5, for examples). "Gehenna" was a valley on the edge of Jerusalem; folks knew it as the site of ancient sacrifices and now as a burning garbage dump for the city. Being separated from God is like ending up in the garbage heap. Jesus' listeners would grasp that picture!

It is not up to us to decide who goes to hell (Matt. 7:1; Rom. 14:4). We have confidence that God is able to judge rightly (Gen. 18:25). In Jesus Christ, God has offered access to eternal community with God, and those who in free will say "No" to that offer suffer the punishment of separation (1 Thess. 1:9–10). But God can make us worthy (in righteousness) of the call to be with the righteous God (1 Thess. 1:11).

> Jesus! The name high over all, in hell or earth or sky;
> angels and mortals prostrate fall, and devils fear and fly.

Another question: If God is so loving, why is there a hell?

65. What do United Methodists teach about sin?

This question about sin comes in the chapter on the reign of God because sin is whatever interrupts, opposes, or delays the reign of God. Questions 20 and 21 introduced the topic of sin.

The Wesleyan instruction on salvation (what he calls "the analogy of faith") always includes sin. (What is the meaning of salvation if there is no sin?) The doctrine of sin is part of the essence of Christianity. John Wesley went so far as to say that a doctrine of sin is "one grand, fundamental difference between Christianity . . . and the most refined heathenism" (*Works*, vol. 2, p. 182). Sin is part of the human condition, the human predicament. And what if nothing is done about it? Perhaps the note written in a family Bible by Jacob Albright (founder of the Evangelical Association) brings into focus the issue of doing nothing about sin: "Much better never born, than to be forever lost." A sinner is lost (Rom. 6:23; James 1:15; Rev. 21:8).

There is a universal need for the forgiveness that God gives through justifying grace (Rom. 3:23–24; Eph. 2:8–10). Forgiveness for what? God's prevenient grace (see question 25) uses the law to convince us of our sin (Gal. 3:23–24; Matt. 5:17; Acts 13:39). Wesley understood "law" to be more than the ceremonial and ritual laws of the Old Testament and more than the Mosaic law (Ten Commandments—Exod. 20:1–17). For Wesley, the law was captured by Jesus in the Sermon on the Mount (Matt. 5:1–12; thirteen of the fifty-three sermons in Wesley's standard collection are on the Sermon on the Mount). The law is, in essence, "love God and love neighbor." They are the first and second great commandments (Matt. 22:36–40). It is the failure to love God and neighbor that defines our separation from God, our sin.

Strangely enough, God's love for us is made most evident because we are sinners (Rom. 5:8)! Does that mean that we ought to sin a little extra so God will love us a little extra (Rom. 6:1)? No! God's will is that we be freed from the guilt of sin (justification) and from the power of sin (sanctification). By the justifying and sanctifying grace of God (see question 25) sin is no longer in charge; the Spirit in Christ Jesus has set the believer free from the law of sin and death (Rom. 8:2), and the reign of God is restored.

Where shall my wondering soul begin? How shall I all to heaven aspire?
A slave redeemed from death and sin, a brand plucked from eternal fire, how shall I equal triumphs raise, and sing my great deliverer's praise?

Another question: What is the relationship between law and gospel?

66. What will happen at the end of the world?

The doctrine of last things is called eschatology. (Now there is a good word to try to work into your next conversation in a long line at the supermarket!) "Eschatology" comes from two Greek words— doesn't everything seem to come from two Greek words?!—meaning "talk about the farthest."

It is an exercise of human ego to speak of the end of the world as "last things." With God there are no last things. The ultimate reign of God is about a new beginning (Rev. 21:1, 5). It is what Wesley calls "a new and eternal state of things." The end of the world, then, is really about the full reign of God.

Many in the early church thought Jesus would return soon and institute the new age (see question 12). A few even stopped working because they saw no need to buy groceries if the day of the Lord was at hand (2 Thess. 3:6–12). Even Paul thought there was a good chance that the Parousia (see question 12) would happen during the present generation (1 Cor. 15:51). It did not happen.

So, then, it was time for plan B. If Jesus is not returning right now to establish the day of the Lord, what should we do in the meantime? (The joke is that a bishop told her pastors that if Jesus were to return, be sure to look busy!) The advice that Paul gave to Archippus is good advice: "See that you complete the task that you have received in the Lord" (Col. 4:17). The task for us is to move from the new birth (see question 28) on toward perfection in holiness (see question 23). As we wait during these between-the-times days, we are to be going on to perfection (Ps. 18:30; Matt. 5:48; Phil. 3:12; Jas. 1:17).

We have some clues as to what the new age will look like (Matt. 25:31–46; 1 Cor. 15:54; Eph. 1:21; Col. 1:20; Rev. 21:27). But how will we know when it is about to come? What will be the signs of the end of this age and the beginning of God's new age?

Before beginning some response to that question, it is helpful to read Acts 1:7 ("not for you to know") and Matthew 24:36 ("only the Father" knows) and Deuteronomy 29:29 (God has some secrets). After listing a series of things that will not be the end (Matt. 24:3–12), Jesus says the end of the age will be after the good news has been "proclaimed throughout the world" (Matt. 24:14). (John Wesley thought Jesus was referring here to the destruction of Jerusalem and the temple, which happened in 70 CE.) Even so, the Parousia did not happen in 70 CE.

What about the strange world seen in the book of Revelation or the chaotic visions unfolded in the book of Daniel? Most of these writings are apocalyptic literature, material that is supposed to reveal or unveil what is normally hidden. The style of apocalyptic work is radical imagery given in a time of great persecution. The ultimate purpose is to paint hope and victory with a large, vibrant brush. These scriptural insights do just that, so we too get excited about the full arrival of God's reign. No wonder we join those who cry, "Come, Lord Jesus!" (Rev. 22:20). The only thing to add is the final verse of the Bible (Rev. 22:21): "The grace of the Lord Jesus be with all the saints. Amen."

> "Rejoice in glorious hope! Jesus the Judge shall come,
> and take his servants up to their eternal home.
> We soon shall hear th'archangel's voice;
> the trump of God shall sound, rejoice!

Another question: What difference would it make in your life if you knew precisely when the world as we know it will end?

12

History and Heritage

6/23

67. Who was John Wesley (and who were all these others)?

United Methodists believe God acts in history, so the stories and accounts of the men and women who have forged the United Methodist experience are important. Given a time line that goes back over three hundred years, and given the fact that now there are almost eight million United Methodists in the United States and almost two million in other countries, it is a bit tricky—if not nervy!—to identify a mere handful for inclusion in this chapter! To get started, let me sketch a brief word picture of each of the five men who are considered founders of the movements that merged into United Methodism. To minimize upset stomachs among United Methodist people, I'll do it alphabetically!

Jacob Albright (1759–1808): He was a Lutheran farmer and tile maker in Pennsylvania. After a religious conversion under the ministry of a lay Methodist preacher, Albright led a group of German-speaking Christians in forming religious societies that over time led to the establishment of the Evangelical Association.

Martin Boehm (1725–1812): He was a Mennonite farmer who was chosen (by lot) to be a pastor. His religious fervor increased as he expanded evangelistic work among German-speaking people in Pennsylvania and as he cooperated with Methodist preachers in English-speaking settings. His work led to the founding of the Church of the United Brethren in Christ.

Philip William Otterbein (1726–1813): He was a highly educated Reformed pastor in Germany who answered a call in 1752 to minister to German-speaking people in America. In theology and polity and friendships he was close to the Methodist movement. Out of his leadership (along with Boehm), a German revival movement helped shaped the beginning of the United Brethren in Christ Church.

Charles Wesley (1707–1788): He was one of two brothers whose commitment to holy living led to the Methodist revival in England. As a priest in the Church of England, he had solid theological training. One of his great gifts of ministry was in expressing the gospel in doctrinally sound hymns—he wrote over six thousand.

John Wesley (1703–1791): He was the older of the two brothers who sparked an evangelical and sacramental revival in the Church of England. A priest loyal to the Church of England, he finally saw the need for the separation of the American expression of the movement and authorized the organization of the Methodist Episcopal Church in America.

In 1922, the Evangelical Church was formed out of several branches that had come out of the original ministries of Jacob Albright. In 1800, followers of Martin Boehm and Philip William Otterbein organized the Church of the United Brethren in Christ. Its journey included divisions and expansions until the Evangelical Church and the Church of the United Brethren in Christ merged in 1946 as the Evangelical United Brethren Church.

The Methodist Episcopal Church in America (1784) had its own splits and crises, but in 1939 three major streams (Methodist Episcopal Church; Methodist Episcopal Church, South; and Methodist Protestant Church) reunited as The Methodist Church.

In 1968, the Evangelical United Brethren and The Methodist Church celebrated much common history, similar missional foci, and mutual evangelical thrust by uniting as The United Methodist Church.

> And are we yet alive, and see each other's face?
> Glory and thanks to Jesus give for his almighty grace!

Another question: What has been gained and what has been lost as various reunions and mergers have created The United Methodist Church?

68. What are the different types of Methodists?

There are Methodists who are not United Methodists. Roots for these various Methodist families are in the Wesleyan movement in eighteenth-century England. Many of these denominations are part of the World Methodist Council, an association of people in the Methodist tradition throughout the world. Although the World Methodist Council seeks to give unity to the work of Methodists, it has no legislative authority and does not invade the autonomy of its member bodies. Its statement of purpose includes words such as "deepen," "foster," "advance," "suggest," "promote," "encourage," "study," and "assist."

It is unfair to persons who came from the Evangelical United Brethren Church to use the term "Methodist" when referring solely to The United Methodist Church. It is also unfair to other branches of Methodism to assume that the title "Methodist Church" applies only to The United Methodist Church. Who are some of these other Methodist people?

African Methodist Episcopal Church (1816): the A.M.E. Church emerged under the leadership of Richard Allen as a protest in Philadelphia against second-class treatment of black members of the Methodist Episcopal Church

African Methodist Episcopal Zion Church (1796): the A.M.E. Zion Church developed in New York City and was led by James Varick as a movement for black members who removed themselves from the Methodist Episcopal Church to avoid racist treatment.

The Methodist Church of Great Britain (1795): Methodism was officially organized in England after the death of John Wesley and after the structure of the Methodist Episcopal Church in America; its present form took shape in a 1932 reunion of several divisions.

The Methodist Church in Mexico (1930): After years of missionary work from the United States, Methodists in Mexico became an autonomous denomination, Iglesia Metodista de Mexico.

The Wesleyan Church (1968): This denomination united the Pilgrim Holiness Church (1897) and the Wesleyan Church of America (1843). Strong antislavery opinions and an emphasis on sanctification led these groups away from the Methodist Episcopal Church.

Church of the Nazarene (1908): Predecessor groups of the Church of the Nazarene formed when they felt the Methodist Episcopal Church was losing its emphasis on entire sanctification.

Christian Methodist Episcopal Church (1870): The C.M.E. Church was first known as the Colored Methodist Episcopal Church. Isaac Lane led the growth of this denomination as former slaves sought a church independent of the Methodist Episcopal Church, South.

Free Methodist Church (1860): B. T. Roberts helped establish this fellowship after feeling that other expressions of Methodism had abandoned the original Wesleyan teachings, particularly entire sanctification.

Around the world there are close to 40,000,000 persons who identify themselves as Methodists (only a fourth of them members of The United Methodist Church). About double that number see themselves as part of a Methodist community. United Methodists have lots of cousins!

> Love, like death, hath all destroyed, rendered all distinctions void; names and sects and parties fall; thou, O Christ, art all in all!

Another question: What are distinguishing marks for "people called Methodist"?

 69. How did United Methodism get to the United States?

Because The United Methodist Church was not founded until 1968, a better way to ask this question is, "How did the roots of United Methodism get to the United States?"

Philip William Otterbein (see question 67) came with five others from Germany in 1752 to expand ministry among German-speaking people, primarily in Pennsylvania and Maryland. He brought with him a passion for Bible study, small prayer groups, and preaching of the new birth in Christ. The family of Martin Boehm (see question 67) had come to this country in 1715 to escape religious persecution. His ministry was marked by great zeal and a call to pious living. Jacob Albright (see question 67) was probably a second-generation American. Among German-speaking persons in

Pennsylvania, he spoke of conversion and the value of fellowship among believers. A review of the influence of these three key leaders shows some of the first fruit of United Methodist values in this country.

Lay Methodists from England and Ireland brought their passion for the gospel to the colonies. Persons such as Robert Strawbridge, Philip Embury, Barbara Heck, and Thomas Webb set the pace. John Wesley (see question 67) sought to strengthen the work by sending experienced lay preachers: Richard Boardman, Joseph Pilmore, Richard Wright, and Francis Asbury (see question 70).

Methodists in America hungered for regular access to the Lord's Supper, but there were no ordained clergy to preside at the Table. John Wesley sought to get authorities in the Church of England to send priests to America for the Methodist people, but they would not. After study, Wesley came to understand that the New Testament office of elder (priest) and the New Testament office of bishop were the same (see question 34). In light of that, he himself a priest, and not a bishop, with the laying on of hands set apart Richard Whatcoat and Thomas Vasey as ordained clergy and set apart Thomas Coke as general superintendent of the American ministry (with the instruction that Francis Asbury was to be afforded the same responsibility). This action by John Wesley made it possible for the Methodists in America to become an independent church. The "practical divinity" (see question 51) of United Methodism was well planted on American soil.

When at a Christmas conference in 1784 Francis Asbury (see question 70) was ordained and set apart as a general superintendent (bishop), among those who joined in the laying on of hands was Philip William Otterbein (see question 67). How wonderfully God began to bring together the inheritance of The United Methodist Church!

> Joined in one spirit to our Head, where he appoints we go,
> and still in Jesus' footsteps tread, and do his work below.

Another question: Which part of United Methodist history most deeply needs to be recovered?

7©. Who were Francis Asbury and Christian Newcomer and Harry Hosier?

These three names represent scores of men and women—both heralded and unknown—who had shaping influence on the forerunners of today's United Methodist Church. A quick telling of the story of a few of these brothers and sisters in the faith will give some view of the "great . . . cloud of witnesses" (Heb. 12:1).

Francis Asbury (1745–1816) was one of the first general superintendents for Methodist work in America (along with Thomas Coke). Affirming that a shepherd does not leave his sheep, Asbury was the only English preacher who stayed (sometimes in hiding!) in this country during the Revolutionary War. His evangelistic travels as a circuit rider made him a hands-on leader for the rapidly growing Methodist work. The retail arm of the United Methodist Publishing House is named Cokesbury after the first two bishops—Coke and Asbury.

Christian Newcomer (1749–1830) was initially resistant to the idea of preaching, but came under the influence of Otterbein and Boehm (see question 67) and began a ministry of almost fifty years. He kept a careful journal, which records nearly two hundred thousand miles on horseback as he worked as an evangelist, pastor, and early organizer of the United Brethren Church. One of his principle contributions was writing doctrinal and organizational statements.

Harry Hosier (1750–1806) was a riding companion of Bishop Asbury. Hosier (sometimes spelled "Hoosier") was a freed slave; he became known as an extraordinary preacher. Some accounts indicate that he was the first African American to be licensed to preach in American Methodism. Although the Methodist appeal to the poor and outcast helped them in ministry among the slaves, Harry Hosier's power and attraction went far beyond the black Methodists. Some even wondered if Bishop Asbury might have been a little jealous of Hosier's preaching prowess! Harry Hosier was present at the conference that organized American Methodism in 1784.

Barbara Heck (1734–1804) helped form the first Methodist society in New York in 1766. She had come from Ireland and brought an enthusiasm for bringing together people to hear strong preaching and an eagerness to improve the moral life of those around her. Barbara Heck was among a group of British loyalists who migrated to Canada as the new United States began to solidify. There, she and her husband, Paul, assisted in promulgating a strong Methodist presence that continues today in The United Church of Canada.

George Miller (1774–1816) grew up in a devout Lutheran home. In 1798, he heard Jacob Albright (see question 67) preach, and within a few years, at the risk of loss of family and the retaliatory destruction of his livelihood as a miller, he began an energetic traveling ministry. Once health forced him to stop circuit riding, he undertook a ministry of writing. Basing his work on the Methodist *Book of Discipline*, he devised articles of faith and a *Book of Discipline* for the Evangelical Association.

Where is such an account to stop? Should we note Susannah Wesley? What about John Walter or John George Pfrimmer or the Wyandotte Between-the-Logs or Alejo Hernández or Hon Fan Chan or Sojourner Truth or Charity Opherel or . . . ? God continues to raise up leaders among United Methodists.

> We all are one who him receive, and each with each agree,
> in him the One, the Truth, we live; blest point of unity!

Another question: How do United Methodist leaders differ from each other and what do they seem to have in common?

71. Who was Marjorie Matthews?

In 1980, United Methodist Marjorie Swank Matthews became the first woman elected bishop in any "mainline" denomination. The road to full clergy rights and responsibilities for women has not been a smooth one, but now almost 25 percent of United Methodist clergy are women.

The early church had women who prayed and prophesied (1 Cor. 11:5). The New Testament church had women in roles of leadership (Euodia, Syntyche, Mary, Prisca, Tryphosa, Junia, Tryphaena, Lydia, Dorcas, to name a few). There is biblical record (Rom. 16:1–2) of a woman serving as a deacon. In John Wesley's *Explanatory Notes*, there is this comment on 1 Corinthians 11:11: "Neither [male nor female] is excluded; neither is preferred before the other in [God's] kingdom."

In 1761, Sarah Crosby became the first woman licensed by John Wesley to preach. In 1787, the Methodist conference in England authorized Sarah Mallett to preach. Ordination was another matter. It was not until 1866 that any predecessor of United Methodism ordained a woman; in that year, the North Indiana Conference of the Methodist Protestant Church (prior to its full affiliation with the Methodist Protestant Church) ordained Helenor M. Davison. Pauline Martindale, Maggie Ritchie Elliott, and Anna Howard Shaw were also soon ordained in the Methodist Protestant tradition.

In The United Brethren Church, Charity Opheral was commended to preach in 1847. Lydia Sexton was licensed to preach in 1859. The 1889 General Conference of The United Brethren Church voted clergy rights for women. Until its merger with The United Brethren Church in 1946, the Evangelical Church had no practice of ordaining women.

The Methodist Church waited until 1956 to grant full clergy rights to women (although some had been serving as licensed pastors). Maude Jensen of the Central Pennsylvania conference was the first to be received into full conference membership as a clergywoman.

The United Methodist Church now gives full clergy status to women on the same basis as men. Local church committees on lay personnel (nominating committees) are encouraged to include both women and men in roles of lay leadership. Although strides have been made toward the New Testament vision of equality (Gal. 3:28), there continue to be reports of resistance to women as pastors and church leaders. One of the tragedies of the sin of sexism is that a woman whose leadership is not respected cannot be sure whether it is because she is a woman or because of some limitation in her personal gifts and grace. Maybe it is time to listen again to Susannah Wesley (mother of John and Charles). While her husband, Samuel, was away from his duties as rector of St. Andrew's Church in Epworth, Susannah held evening services, and many in the parish came. Samuel asked her to stop. Susannah said, only if you send me "your positive command." In that way, she concluded, I shall be absolved "from all guilt and punishment for neglecting this opportunity of doing good to souls, when you and I shall appear before the great and awful tribunal of our Lord Jesus Christ." Samuel got the message. The services continued.

> Stand then in his great might, with all his strength endued,
> but take to arm you for the fight the panoply of God;
> that having all things done, and all your conflicts passed,
> ye may o'ercome thru Christ alone and stand entire at last.

Another question: What role have women had in your spiritual journey?

72. How do United Methodists get along with others?

I suppose "others" are the ones to ask!

United Methodists see themselves as part of the larger body of Christ (Col. 1:18). Nothing in the Articles of Religion or in the Confession of Faith (see question 49) indicates that the church of Jesus Christ exists solely in its United Methodist expression.

By maintaining membership in ecumenical agencies, The United Methodist Church declares its desire to move toward Christian unity (John 17:21). The *BOD* identifies a number of these relationships (*BOD*, ¶2404): Churches Uniting in Christ, National Council of the Churches of Christ in the U.S.A., and the World Council of Churches. The United Methodist Church has observer status in the National Association of Evangelicals and seeks such a relationship with the World Evangelical Fellowship. The American Bible Society is recognized as an appropriate instrument of United Methodist mission (¶2405). United Methodism has interim eucharistic sharing agreements with the Evangelical Lutheran Church in America and with The Episcopal Church. There are ongoing dialogues with these bodies, with churches in the Reformed tradition, with other Methodist denominations (see question 68), and with the Roman Catholic Church. Through the General Commission on Christian Unity and Interreligious Concerns (*BOD*, ¶2404.3b), the denomination seeks dialogue with other non-Christian faith groups. It is as if there is an effort to understand the echo of Acts 10:28: ". . . but God has shown me that I should not call anyone profane or unclean."

One way The United Methodist Church has good faith recognition of other Christian families is a provision that allows ordained clergy from other denominations to serve United Methodist congregations (*BOD*, ¶346.2) if they, among other things, are in agreement with United Methodist doctrine, discipline, and polity. If a pastor from another denomination is admitted for transfer into The United Methodist Church, her or his previous ordination is recognized as valid and there is no additional "United Methodist ordination" (*BOD*, ¶348).

In a sermon on "Catholic Spirit" (*Works*, vol. 2, pp. 81–95), John Wesley calls for Christians to cease squabbles about things that are not essentials of the faith. Wesley is clear that this does not mean an indifference to opinion (Wesley used the charming term "speculative latitudinarianism." I can't recall the last time I used those words in daily conversation!) The catholic spirit—remember "catholic" means "universal"—reflects "one who . . . gives his hand to all whose hearts are right with his heart." In that tone, United Methodists feel at home in a variety of denominational settings and have an open hand, ready to extend.

Come, and let us sweetly join, Christ to praise in hymns divine;
give we all with one accord glory to our common Lord.

Another question: How do the many denominations form one body of Christ?

13

Polity

 73. What is *The Book of Discipline*?

In brief, *The Book of Discipline* (frequently referred to as *BOD* in this study) is the book of law for The United Methodist Church. It is how United Methodists seek to be disciples ("disciple" and "discipline" have the same root). It is a covenant among United Methodist people to hold one another accountable to our common heritage, our theological undergirding, our biblical faith, our connectional nature, and our missional task. How will we do all that? The answer in the 2004 edition runs over seven hundred pages!

Each of the merged tributaries that make up United Methodism has long employed such a plan for life together. Growing out of the Minutes kept at the conferences John Wesley held in England, the Methodist Episcopal Church in America in 1785 published *The Doctrines and Discipline of The Methodist Episcopal Church in America.* In 1808, the United Brethren in Christ Church translated the Methodist *Discipline* into German; in 1813, the United Brethren called for publication of their own *Discipline.* The Evangelical Association adopted *The Articles of Faith and the Book of Discipline* in 1809. It drew heavily on a German translation of the Methodist *Discipline.*

The United Methodist *Book of Discipline* is revised every four years by the actions of the worldwide General Conference (see question 74). Restrictive rules in the denomination's Constitution draw a box around six items that cannot be revoked or changed: (a) the Articles of Religion (see question 49); (b) the Confession of Faith (see question 49); (c) the office of general superintendency;

(d) clergy and lay members' right to church trial; (e) General Rules (see question 31); (f) use of publishing house profit for anything other than retired or disabled clergy and their families.

Although the pages of *The Book of Discipline* are numbered, reference to particular items is usually made by identifying the relevant paragraph number. For example, membership and organization of a local church board of trustees is addressed in *BOD*, ¶2529. (*Discipline*-toting United Methodists consider the fact that the paragraph begins on page 687 as irrelevant! In some circles, it is considered a badge of honor to be able to throw out paragraph references by number as if everyone present knows what the paragraph says; I mean you *do* know the subject matter of ¶703.7c, don't you? If not, you can sneak a look at page 454!) Because *The Book of Discipline* changes every four years, it is important to have access to the most recent edition.

United Methodists agree to live by *The Book of Discipline*, even if at the same time they are working to get it changed! In fact, it is a chargeable offense (subject to trial, which is quite rare) for either a clergyperson or a layperson to be "disobedient to the Order and Discipline of The United Methodist Church" (*BOD*, ¶2702). Church discipline (lowercase "d") is important because faithful discipleship is how we give honor to God. In the United Methodist tradition, we need each other in the connection to help us understand what this means and to support us in carrying out those disciplines. Church membership is not a solo sport!

> To serve the present age, my calling to fulfill;
> O may it all my powers engage to do my Master's will!

Another question: How might *The Book of Discipline* help a person be a disciple of Jesus Christ?

74. What is a conference?

From the days of Wesley, Otterbein, and Albright, and through the times of painful division and the times of pure delight, United Methodists in all their configurations have been a people of conference (Acts 15:6). The very word "conference" reflects the United

Methodist understanding that God has chosen us for a connected community, one that confers, one that decides together, one that holds each responsible to the other, one that seeks to do together what can best be done together (see question 31). United Methodism exists in a series of interrelated conferences.

Charge conference: This is an annual (or called) meeting for the elected leaders of a local church (or occasionally, for the entire congregation). It connects the local church to the rest of United Methodism; the district superintendent (or an elder named by the superintendent) presides. At this meeting, officers are elected, property matters are handled, reports and plans for ministry are exchanged, and oversight is given of the church council (which handles the day-to-day administrative and spiritual affairs of the local church). If more than one local church is served by the same pastor, these churches come together for the charge conference. The charge conference recommends persons who seek to be candidates for ordained ministry.

District conference: If an annual conference requires it, churches in a region (called a district) meet for district business. (A few districts are organized by congregational demographics rather than geography.) The role of the district varies around United Methodism.

Annual conference: The annual conference is the basic body of the church. Here clergy members and lay members (elected at charge conference) come together to vote on proposed changes to the Constitution, to elect delegates to jurisdictional/central and General conferences, to name those who are to be appointed, to approve those to be ordained, to plan for common financial and programmatic life, and to hear the pastoral appointments for the ensuing year. The geographic size of annual conferences varies around the world; in the United States there are sixty-four annual conferences, but the number changes as mergers and expansions occur.

Jurisdictional/central conference: In the United States, larger regional bodies (five for the entire country) are called jurisdictional conferences. Outside the United States, these entities are called central conferences (seven around the world, although that number can change). Although the conferences at this level do varying amounts of program ministry, their main assignment is the quadrennial (every four years) election of bishops (see question 76). Delegates to the jurisdictional and central conferences are elected by annual conferences.

General Conference: Every four years, United Methodists from around the world come as delegates to the General Conference. In addition to revising, clarifying, and editing *The Book of Discipline*, the delegates (chosen by annual conferences) set missional goals, determine organizational patterns, decide financial apportionments, and make statements on behalf of the entire denomination. Only the General Conference can speak for The United Methodist Church. The membership is limited to one thousand or fewer, with each annual conference getting its number of delegates (equally lay and clergy), based on a formula that roughly reflects membership totals.

Sleep with this under your pillow tonight. I'm sure it will make more sense in the morning.

> Refining fire, go through my heart, illuminate my soul;
> scatter thy life through every part and sanctify the whole.

Another question: What does it mean for a United Methodist to say, "Conference is not *they*; conference is *we*"?

75. What is the trust clause?

The trust clause in deeds is one way that United Methodists say, "We are in this together." The practice goes back to the days of Wesley and was part of the polity (organization) of both the Evangelical United Brethren Church and The Methodist Church. Basically, the trust clause (required in all deeds of property owned by denominational entities, including local churches) states that property is held in trust for the denomination. There are two chief practical implications of this policy: (1) the district (see question 74) committee on church location and building must approve financial and architectural plans for local church construction and (2) if a local church ceases to be a United Methodist congregation, the property becomes the responsibility of the annual conference board of trustees.

It is not correct to say that "the conference owns our building," as some United Methodists think. The property is under the control of the local church (according to the *BOD*) as long as that local church is United Methodist. The effect of the clause is activated only if the local church is abandoned or chooses to leave the denomination. The trust clause is considered included in deeds (even if the words are not) if any of the following is true: (1) the property was conveyed to a United Methodist entity; (2) the entity—local church, for example—presents itself to the community as United Methodist by use of "name, customs, and polity of The United Methodist Church"; or (3) the local church accepts pastors appointed by the bishop or employed by the district superintendent.

Wesley developed deeds that protected Methodist property from those persons who would try to use that property for practices that were contrary to Methodist doctrine and custom. The Deed of Declaration in 1784 gave the "Legal Hundred" (a forerunner of today's annual conference) the same authority that John and Charles Wesley had during their lifetimes. A "model deed" was written, a precursor of today's trust clause. Such deed assures anyone who gives a gift for United Methodist property that such property will always be tied to the United Methodist connection. In a sense, any United Methodist can pass by any United Methodist property and say, joyfully, "Hey! That's ours too!"

In the twenty-first century, complex legal issues surface as civil courts try to untangle property matters involving connectional denominations such as The United Methodist Church. At the time of this writing, there is a major study underway to try to maintain the intent of the trust clause within the context of today's civil legal codes. Stay tuned.

If you find your appetite irresistibly whetted by this discussion of the trust clause, you can read the stuff for yourself in *BOD*, ¶s 2501–2505.

> Glory to God, and praise and love be ever, ever given,
> by saints below and saints above, the church in earth and heaven.

Another question: How does the trust clause protect the United Methodist witness to Christ?

76. How are bishops chosen, and what do they do?

Bishops are the general superintendents of The United Methodist Church. Elected for life, they serve until retirement in areas to which they are assigned by the jurisdictional or central conference (see question 74). District superintendents are elders (see question 34) in full connection who are appointed by the bishop as an extension of the bishop's office. The district superintendents serve smaller regions within the bishop's area. The bishop and superintendents form the cabinet; for nonappointive work, they are joined by others who by virtue of office are designated members of an extended cabinet. (For example, an extended cabinet might include the conference treasurer, the conference lay leader, and an assistant to the bishop. The makeup is not the same in each area.)

Bishops are elected by the delegates at a jurisdictional or central conference. Usually, candidates are nominated by annual conferences, but any elder in the full connection is eligible for election (1 Tim. 3:1). In The United Methodist Church, bishops are not ordained to a third order as they are in Roman Catholic, Orthodox, and Anglican communions; they remain elders. The *BOD* recommends that a candidate receive 60 percent of the votes cast (lay and clergy voting together) in order to be elected.

The number of bishops is determined by a formula established by the General Conference. At the present time, there are nineteen active bishops outside the United States, fifty active bishops in the United States, and ninety-four retired bishops (who have voice but not vote in the Council of Bishops). Bishops are general superintendents for the whole denomination which means that while they are assigned to an area of residence, they also serve the whole church. Individually and collectively, bishops bear responsibility for the spiritual and temporal life of the church (Titus 1:7–9). They are signs of the unity of the church and are expected to teach the church (Acts 15:22–30). The Council of Bishops is the collegial expression of episcopal leadership.

The bishops preside (but have no vote) at the annual, jurisdictional, central, and General conferences. After consultation with pastors and local churches (through pastor–parish relations committees) and with the advice of the district superintendents, the bishops appoint the clergy to their places of service (see question 78). The bishop of an area has oversight of the process of handling formal complaints against clergy or laity and monitors the fairness of administrative and judicial proceedings (see question 77). In The United Methodist Church, bishops ordain elders and deacons (see question 34) and consecrate newly elected bishops. In this role, they act on behalf of the whole church.

I would the precious time redeem, and longer live for this alone,
to spend and to be spent for them who have not yet my Savior known;
fully on these my mission prove, and only breathe, to breathe thy love.

Another question: How does a bishop express the unity of the church?

77. What are chargeable offenses?

The New Testament calls on the Christian community to build up one another (1 Cor. 10:23; 1 Thess. 5:11). Within the church, we are called to a family covenant of accountability, to help each of us be the best he or she can be. First Peter 4:17 reports that judgment will begin with the household of God. We owe it to one another to alert the sister or brother whose journey has taken that individual off the path toward sanctification! One way we bear that awesome responsibility is through the procedures for chargeable offenses. *BOD*, ¶2702.1 lists those items for which clergy and diaconal ministers may be charged; in ¶2702.2; there is a list of items for which professing members of a local church might be charged. The goal of these processes is always to have a just resolution, seeking reconciliation and healing and justice in the body of Christ. That sounds a lot like the challenge of 1 Corinthians 1:8: "so that you may be blameless on the day of our Lord Jesus Christ."

Both the list for clergy and the list for laity include these offenses that need to be addressed: (a) immorality, (b) crime, (c) disobedience to the Order and Discipline of The United Methodist Church, (d) false teaching, (e) sexual abuse, (f) sexual misconduct, (g) child abuse, (h) harassment, including racial harassment, (i) racial or gender discrimination, and (j) relationships and/or behavior that undermine the ministry of a clergyperson under appointment. For clergy, there are two additional items: (1) failure to do the work of ministry, and (2) practice of homosexuality or conducting ceremonies that celebrate homosexual unions or performing same-sex wedding ceremonies. (In most cases, I have summarized the lists rather than quoting verbatim. See *BOD*, ¶2702.1 and ¶2702.3 for the exact wording.)

If a person is charged with one of these offenses, there are assurances of fair process, including, if the person chooses, a church trial. The steps in resolving complaints against clergy and resolving complaints against laypersons differ. In both cases, before the matter moves to a judicial administration, there is an effort through a supervisory response (or pastoral response) to obtain a just resolution. Church trial is a matter of last resort. Such trials are extremely rare.

More frequently, the complaint can be attended to with peer support and supervision, or counseling and therapy, or a program of continuing education, or a private reprimand, or a number of possible voluntary or involuntary changes in status. Sometimes an accused pastor will voluntarily withdraw from a conference relationship. Or, of course, the bishop can dismiss the complaint, although, in truth, today's fear of things being swept under the rug makes that difficult.

Discipline is not for punishment but for redemption. The question is: In this circumstance, how is the whole church to be strengthened for ministry and mission?

The commitment of the church to truth telling (2 John 1:4) demands that someone who is charged have avenues through which to respond. There is no assumption of guilt. Paul called the church "the pillar and bulwark of the truth" (1 Tim. 3:15). There is no more important ingredient than truth in the mission of building up one another. The message of Psalm 85:10 is that love and truth are kinfolk! Truth makes for peace (Zech. 8:16).

The procedure for making a charge and the importance of responding to a charge are captured in Ephesians 4:15: speaking the truth in love.

Thou hidden source of calm repose, thou all-sufficient love divine,
my help and refuge from my foes, secure I am if thou art mine;
and lo! from sin and grief and shame I hide me, Jesus, in thy name.

Another question: What is the relationship between discipline and love?

 78. Why do the preachers move so often (and other questions that didn't fit in anywhere else)?

John Wesley believed that itinerant preachers who moved from place to place were more effective than those who settled in, grew comfortable, and wore out what they had to say. The length of tenure for United Methodist pastors has gradually increased as contemporary social forces make longer pastorates more fruitful. Even so, United Methodist clergy are all appointed for one year at a time (except for bishops, who are assigned four years at a time).

United Methodist pastors are sent, not called (see question 76). In a connectional church such as United Methodism, the question from any individual congregation or from any individual pastor is not "What is best for me?" The question is "What is best for us, the whole connection?" (See question 36.) The one who has oversight makes those decisions. (Remember: the New Testament word for bishop is *episkopos,* which means the one who can see the whole picture.)

The changing of pastors brings different, and often needed, gifts to the local church (1 Cor. 12:4). The changing of settings can keep a pastor refreshed. The missionary journeys of Paul are surely a reminder of that (for example, Acts 13:2–14:7; 15:36–18:22; 18:23–21:19)!

Another issue: How is The United Methodist Church organized? There is a legislative arm (conference—such as Acts 15:1–6). There is an executive branch (bishops—such as 1 Tim. 3:1–7). There is a judicial focus (Judicial Council—such as Judg. 2:16). This balance of power grows out of a doctrine of sin: Do not let too much power accumulate in any one place.

Power is balanced in other ways: the pastor chairs the committee on lay personnel (nominations), but does not preside when the church council meets. The pastor decides whom to receive into membership but cannot remove someone from membership. The bishop ordains, but the clergy of the conference decide who gets

ordained. The bishop appoints pastors, but the clergy in full connection decide who is to be appointed. The local charge conference
starts persons on the way to ordination, but district and conference
boards on ordained ministry make the final recommendation. There
are equal lay and clergy members of annual, jurisdictional, central,
and General conferences. United Methodism is organized with a
sense of balance.

Local churches have some flexibility to organize in the best ways
to accomplish their mission. The church council is the administrative and programming body. The minimum structure includes a
council chair, a committee on lay leadership, a committee on pas-
tor-parish relations, financial officers and trustees, lay leader, lay
member of annual conference, and a recording secretary. As at all
levels of United Methodism, attention is to be given to racial, gender, age, disability, and theological inclusion.

Another issue: What is the meaning of the cross-and-flame logo
of The United Methodist Church? The cross of Jesus Christ is central, and its emptied message is our salvation; the flames of the Holy
Spirit send us forth to serve in the world. (Some add that the two
flames blend to form one flame, just as the Evangelical United
Brethren Church and The Methodist Church merged to form one
denomination.) Only official United Methodist usage of the image
is permitted.

> Christ, whose glory fills the skies, Christ, the true, the only light,
> Sun of Righteousness, arise, triumph o'er the shades of night;
> Dayspring from on high, be near; Daystar, in my heart appear.

Another question: If you could change one thing about The United
Methodist Church, what would it be?

Hymns Quoted

The quotations at the end of each answer come from the hymns of Charles Wesley. The references given here note the stanza and hymn number where those selections appear in *The United Methodist Hymnal*. For example, "332.1" means the first stanza of hymn 332 and "88.4" means the fourth stanza of hymn 88.

Chapter 1: God

1.	332.1	"Spirit of Faith, Come Down"
2.	88.4	"Maker, in Whom We Live"
3.	561.4	"Jesus, United by Thy Grace"
4.	384.4	"Love Divine, All Loves Excelling"
5.	635.2	"Because Thou Hast Said"
6.	96.3	"Praise the Lord Who Reigns Above"

Chapter 2: Jesus Christ

7.	240.2b	"Hark! the Herald Angels Sing"
8.	240.2a	"Hark! the Herald Angels Sing"
9.	287.1	"O Love Divine, What Hast Thou Done"
10.	363.2	"And Can It Be that I Should Gain"
11.	302.2	"Christ the Lord Is Risen Today"
12.	718.1	"Lo, He Comes with Clouds Descending"

Chapter 3: Holy Spirit

13.	332.2	"Spirit of Faith, Come Down"
14.	603.4	"Come, Holy Ghost, Our Hearts Inspire"

Chapter 3: Holy Spirit (*continued*)
15.	438.1	"Forth in Thy Name, O Lord"
16.	346.3a	"Sinners, Turn: Why Will You Die"
17.	501.1	"O Thou Who Camest from Above"
18.	554.3	"All Praise to Our Redeeming Lord"

Chapter 4: Humanity
19.	88.1	"Maker, in Whom We Live"
20.	355.2	"Depth of Mercy"
21.	388.1	"O Come and Dwell in Me"
22.	384.2b	"Love Divine, All Loves Excelling"
23.	417.4	"O For a Heart to Praise My God"
24.	709.3	"Come, Let Us Join Our Friends Above"

Chapter 5: Salvation
25.	385.1	"Let Us Plead for Faith Alone"
26.	355.5	"Depth of Mercy"
27.	355.3	"Depth of Mercy"
28.	410.3	"I Want a Principle Within"
29.	385.2	"Let Us Plead for Faith Alone"
30.	339.1	"Come, Sinners, to the Gospel Feast"

Chapter 6: Church
31.	550.5	"Christ, from Whom All Blessings Flow"
32.	562.4	"Jesus, Lord, We Look to Thee"
33.	554.4	"All Praise to Our Redeeming Lord"
34.	650.3	"Give Me Faith Which Can Remove"
35.	438.2	"Forth in Thy Name, O Lord"
36.	554.2	"All Praise to Our Redeeming Lord"

Chapter 7: Worship and Sacraments
37.	57.1	"O For a Thousand Tongues to Sing"
38.	627.1	"O the Depths of Love Divine"
39.	627.4	"O the Depths of Love Divine"
40.	606.3	"Come, Let Us Use the Grace Divine"

| 41. | 613.4 | "O Thou, Who This Mysterious Bread" |
| 42. | 96.2 | "Praise the Lord Who Reigns Above" |

Chapter 8: Bible

43.	603.2	"Come, Holy Ghost, Our Hearts Inspire"
44.	595.4b	"Whether the Word Be Preached or Read"
45.	595.1	"Whether the Word Be Preached or Read"
46.	594.1	"Come, Divine Interpreter"
47.	550.2	"Christ, from Whom All Blessings Flow"
48.	541.2	"See How Great a Flame Aspires"

Chapter 9: Theology

49.	181.1	"Ye Servants of God"
50.	193.5	"Jesus! The Name High over All"
51.	196.1	"Come, Thou Long-Expected Jesus"
52.	388.3	"O Come and Dwell in Me"
53.	413.2	"A Charge to Keep I Have"
54.	553.3, 4	"And Are We Yet Alive"*

Chapter 10: Christian Life

55.	479.4	"Jesus, Lover of My Soul"
56.	438.4	"Forth in Thy Name"
57.	501.3	"O Thou Who Camest from Above"
58.	479.3	"Jesus, Lover of My Soul"
59.	449.3	"Our Earth We Now Lament to See"
60.	410.1	"I Want a Principle Within"

Chapter 11: Reign of God

| 61. | 715.1, 3 | "Rejoice, the Lord Is King" |
| 62. | 718.4 | "Lo, He Comes with Clouds Descending" |

---

*This hymn is traditionally sung at the beginning of every United Methodist annual conference.

Chapter 11: Reign of God (*continued*)

63.	385.3	"Let Us Plead for Faith Alone"
64.	193.1	"Jesus! The Name High over All"
65.	342.1	"Where Shall My Wondering Soul Begin"
66.	715.4	"Rejoice, the Lord Is King"

Chapter 12: History and Heritage

67.	553.1	"And Are We Yet Alive"*
68.	550.6	"Christ, from Whom All Blessings Flow"
69.	566.2	"Blest Be the Dear Uniting Love"
70.	566.4	"Blest Be the Dear Uniting Love"
71.	513.2	"Soldiers of Christ, Arise"
72.	699.1	"Come, and Let Us Sweetly Join"

Chapter 13: Polity

73.	413.2	"A Charge to Keep I Have"
74.	422.4	"Jesus, Thine All-Victorious Love"
75.	58.1	"Glory to God, and Praise and Love"
76.	650.2	"Give Me the Faith Which Can Remove"
77.	153.1	"Thou Hidden Source of Calm Repose"
78.	173.1	"Christ, Whose Glory Fills the Skies"

---

*This hymn is traditionally sung at the beginning of every United Methodist annual conference.

For Further Reading

In addition to the source books mentioned on pp. xii–xiii of "Welcome to the Book," you can turn to these items for additional digging.

Abraham, William J. *Wesley for Armchair Theologians*. Louisville, KY: Westminster John Knox Press, 2005.

Albright, Raymond W. *A History of the Evangelical Church*. Harrisburg, PA: Evangelical Press, 1956.

Behney, J. Bruce, and Paul H. Eller. *The History of the Evangelical United Brethren Church*. Edited by Kenneth W. Krueger. Nashville: Abingdon Press, 1979.

Campbell, Ted A. *Methodist Doctrine: The Essentials*. Nashville: Abingdon Press, 1999.

Core, Arthur C. *Philip William Otterbein: Pastor, Ecumenist*. Dayton, OH: Board of Publication of The Evangelical United Brethren Church, 1968.

Gooch, John O. *John Wesley for the 21st Century*. Nashville: Discipleship Resources, 2006.

Heitzenrater, Richard P. *Wesley and the People Called Methodists*. Nashville: Abingdon Press, 1995.

Joyner, F. Belton, Jr. *Being Methodist in the Bible Belt*. Louisville, KY: Westminster John Knox Press, 2004.

Kirby, James E., Russell E. Richey, and Kenneth E. Rowe. *The Methodists*. Westport, CT: Praeger Publishers, 1998.

Klaiber, Walter, and Manfred Marquardt. *Living Grace: An Outline of United Methodist Theology*. Nashville: Abingdon Press, 2001.

Norwood, Frederick A. *The Story of American Methodism*. Nashville: Abingdon Press, 1974.

Stokes, Mack B. *Major United Methodist Beliefs*. Nashville: Abingdon Press, 1989.

Weems, Lovett H. Jr. *John Wesley's Message Today*. Nashville: Abingdon Press, 1991.

You might be interested in exploring United Methodist and Presbyterian similarities and contrasts by reading *Presbyterian Questions, Presbyterian Answers,* by Donald K. McKim (Louisville, KY: Geneva Press, 2003). All these books are available through Cokesbury Bookstores.

Betty's son
Wanda Win.
Sue
Mary's son